THE LIGHT, LEAN, AND LOW-FAT COOKBOOK

CLB 4901

© 1997 by CLB International, a division of Quadrillion Publishing Ltd

Printed and Bound in Italy by New Interlitho Italia S.P.A.

9 8 7 6 5 4 3 2 1
Digit on the right indicates the number of this printing

Library of Congress Cataloging-in-Publication Number 96-69248

ISBN 0-7624-0003-X

This book was designed and produced by CLB International
Godalming, Surrey, England, GU7 1XW

NUTRITIONAL CONSULTANCY by Jill Scott
PROJECT MANAGEMENT by Jo Richardson
PRODUCED by Anthology
ORIGINAL DESIGN CONCEPT by Roger Hyde
DESIGN MANAGEMENT by Rhoda Nottridge
PAGE MAKE-UP by Vanessa Good
PHOTOGRAPHY by Don Last; Sheila Terry — *jacket, pages 12-3, 24-5,*
28-9, 38-9, 44-5, 50-1, 68-9 (home economy by Anne Sheasby)
HOME ECONOMY by Joy Parker and Christine France
AMERICAN ADAPTATION by Josephine Bacon
PRODUCTION DIRECTOR: Gerald Hughes
PRODUCTION by Ruth Arthur, Karen Staff,
Neil Randles, and Paul Randles

Published by Courage Books,
an imprint of Running Press Book Publishers
125 South Twenty-second Street
Philadelphia, Pennsylvania 19103-4399

THE LIGHT, LEAN, AND LOW-FAT COOKBOOK

Anne Sheasby

COURAGE
BOOKS

AN IMPRINT OF RUNNING PRESS
PHILADELPHIA • LONDON

INTRODUCTION

INTRODUCTION

*L*ow-fat diets are recognised to be an important part of a healthy lifestyle, and many of us are changing our eating patterns to help us feel generally more fit, healthy, and energetic. If you enjoy what you eat but would like to improve your diet, then this book is for you.

The Light, Lean, and Low-Fat Cookbook offers delicious, appetizing recipes, based on sound nutritional princples, to satisfy a variety of tastes. It also features easy-to-read information about food, nutrition, and health based on the latest scientific reports, as well as practical advice on nutrition, including how to create an effective and sustainable eating plan for life.

The Light, Lean, and Low-Fat Cookbook is aimed at anyone who wants to make healthy lifestyle changes, and those looking to reduce in particular their calorie and fat intake to enjoy a healthier way of life. It is also an ideal cookbook for those people who want to lose excess weight the healthy way.

The book is aimed at adults and older children, but the principles and recipes are suitable for children over the age of five.

EATING FOR HEALTH

Following a healthy lifestyle is a positive step towards helping yourself make the most of your life. An important part of healthy living is eating the right types of food, to help you feel and look good.

FOOD FACTS
Here are some of the fundamental facts about food and diet:
● Eating the right balance of a variety of different foods is the key to a healthy diet.
● A healthy diet can help protect you and your family from developing heart disease, some cancers, and digestive problems.
● Too many of our calories come from fat in our diet and this can lead to health problems related to excess weight, and increased risk of developing heart disease.
● Eating less fat can actually mean eating more food, not less — but eating the right kinds of foods.

SIX EASY STEPS TO HEALTHY EATING

STEP 1 To ensure your body obtains all the essential nutrients it needs, choose a variety of foods from these groups:
● *starches such as cereals, breads, pasta, rice, and potatoes*
● *fruits and vegetables*
● *milk and other dairy foods*
● *meat, fish, poultry, peas, beans, lentils, nuts, and eggs*

STEP 2 Base your meals around the starchy carbohydrate foods (bread, cereals, pasta, rice, and potatoes) — these foods are low in fat and are a good source of B vitamins and slow-release energy. They should represent the largest serving on your plate.

STEP 3 Aim to eat 5 or more servings of fruits and vegetables every day, and choose different varieties whenever you can. These foods provide valuable vitamins, minerals, and fiber.

STEP 4 Enjoy moderate amounts of meat, fish, poultry, peas, beans, lentils, eggs, and nuts. We tend to eat more of these foods than we really need, but they are important sources of protein, some vitamins, and minerals, especially iron.

STEP 5 Milk and other dairy foods are rich sources of calcium essential for healthy bones. Include low-fat varieties of milk, yogurt, and cheese as part of your daily diet.

STEP 6 Watch out for the "extra" or "occasional" foods such as chocolate, cakes, cookies, and many snacks, such as potato chips. These foods are often packed with fat and sugar, and lead to excess weight gain. Use the recipes in the following chapters for low-fat healthy and tasty alternatives.

FAT FACTS

Here are some important messages about fat in your diet.
- A small amount of fat in the diet is essential for good health and can add flavor and texture to some foods.
- Too much fat, especially saturated fat, can increase the level of cholesterol in your blood and so increase the risk of heart disease.
- Saturated fats are found mainly in animal products such as full-fat dairy products, fatty meats, cream, butter, and products containing these. They are also "hidden" in other foods, including cakes, cookies, pastries, candy, and potato chips.
- Unsaturated fats include two main types: polyunsaturates and monounsaturates. These fats work in different ways in your body. Research shows that polyunsaturated fat helps reduce the level of harmful cholesterol in the blood. Polyunsaturates are found in vegetable oils and fat spreads made from these, whole-grain cereals, nuts, and seeds. A type of polyunsaturated fat is also found in oil-rich fish such as salmon, mackerel, and sardines. This type of fat can help reduce blood clotting and so help protect against heart disease.
- Monounsaturated fat also helps lower levels of harmful cholesterol, and at the same time increases the level of useful cholesterol, helping to protect against heart disease. Monounsaturates are found in olive and canola oils and fat spreads made from these oils.
- As part of your healthy eating plan, aim to limit your intake of all fats, and when you do use fats, use mainly poly or monounsaturated varieties for good health.

THE LIGHT, LEAN, AND LOW-FAT DIET FOR LIFE

The recipes in this book will help you to take practical steps to lower your fat intake, with mouthwatering ideas for every meal. But eating less fat does not mean eating less food, nor compromising on taste. The serving suggestions include ideas for boosting your intake of starchy carbohydrate foods and raw or lightly cooked vegetables. These ingredients, combined with the low-fat dishes, help to shift the focus away from more fatty foods, and ensure a healthy balance of essential nutrients.

Fat is a very concentrated source of energy, and therefore it is easy to eat too much of it. Experts recommend that we limit the percentage of calories from fat, and especially saturated fat, for good health. For most people, this means cutting down on fat and eating more foods rich in starchy carbohydrate, to make up for lost calories. This is true even for people trying to lose weight.

The recommendations are that no more than 30-35% of your calorie intake should come from the total amount of fat in your diet, with no more than 10% from saturated fat. Although this applies to the overall diet, it can also be applied to indivual foods and dishes that make up part of the overall diet. All the recipes in this book have been devised

with this in mind, but remember that the balance of foods you eat with these dishes over a day or week contributes to your healthy diet. Here are some additional and practical hints and tips for achieving a healthy eating pattern.

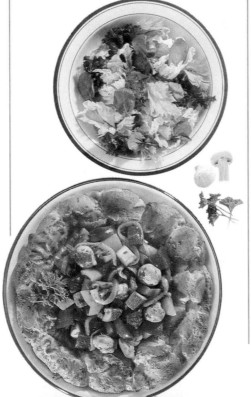

- Eat regularly and try not to skip meals, especially breakfast. A light cereal or fruit (see Chapter 1) is enough to boost your energy level for the day ahead.
- Try to spread your food intake through-out the day, including lunch, rather than have one large meal in the evening. If you prefer, eat small, light meals more often throughout the day (see Chapter 1-3) but watch out for high-fat/high-sugar snacks between meals; opt for fruits, vegetables, and low-fat yogurt, or complex carbohydrates, e.g. toast, English muffin, or fatless cakes.
- Choose whole-wheat/whole-grain varieties of bread, pasta, rice, and breakfast cereals. These are higher in fiber and generally contain more vitamins and minerals than refined varieties.
- Choose low-fat options of staple foods whenever you can, such as low-fat milk, yogurt, and lean meat. Peas, beans, and lentils are naturally low in fat, so try to include these foods more often.
- Drink plenty of fluids every day — at least 8 average glasses or cups — and choose water, fruit juice, low-sugar varieties of carbonated drinks, tea, and coffee (in moderate amounts).
- Eating high-fat foods once in a while is fine; it is what you eat day in, day out that is important for good health.

REDUCING FAT AND CALORIES
IN EVERYDAY MEALS

There are many ways in which you can reduce the fat content of everyday meals and eat a more healthy balance of foods, which can help to improve your general health and well-being. One simple way to reduce your fat intake is to replace full-fat ingredients such as butter, cheese, and sour or heavy cream with reduced-fat ingredients.

By replacing one full-fat ingredient such as cream for a similar, "lighter" ingredient, you will also be able to reduce the fat and therefore calorie content of a meal without affecting the flavor.

Three fairly typical meals have been chosen here and featured in pairs. Each pair of meals consists of an "original" recipe, which is made using more traditional ingredients, and a "lighter" version of the same recipe, which uses alternative fat-reduced ingredients or healthier cooking methods.

As you can see, the recipes within each pair do not differ very much in appearance, but the fat contents and therefore the calorie contents are surprisingly different. The lighter recipe in each case illustrates just how easy it is to make a few simple changes when preparing recipes or cooking food, resulting in quite remarkable fat and calorie savings.

For each pair of meals, there is a panel of points summarizing the ways in which fat and calories have been saved or reduced with only relatively minor changes to the original recipe. Sometimes you will even get a larger portion of food with the lighter recipe, which can't be a bad option!

(original recipe)

Slices of avocado and shrimp have been dressed with a flavored mayonnaise and served on a bed of shredded lettuce.

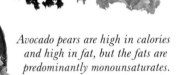

Avocado pears are high in calories and high in fat, but the fats are predominantly monounsaturates.

AVOCADO & SHRIMP COCKTAIL

(lighter recipe)

(full recipe on page 31)

Half the amount of avocado has been used for this recipe. It has been diced and mixed with some cucumber, green onions (scallions), and green bell pepper together with the shrimp.

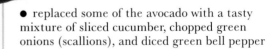

A low-fat yogurt dressing replaces the mayonnaise dressing.

Shrimp are low in fat and are also a good source of protein and some B vitamins.

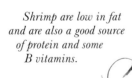

HOW WE REDUCED CALORIES AND FAT

● replaced some of the avocado with a tasty mixture of sliced cucumber, chopped green onions (scallions), and diced green bell pepper

● made a delicious dressing using low-fat yogurt combined with a little tomato ketchup, honey, chopped fresh coriander (cilantro), and a dash of Tabasco sauce. Chili, ground coriander (cilantro), cumin, or crushed fresh garlic may be added to vary the flavor of the dressing

Calories saved = 217 calories per serving

Fat saved = 25.7 g fat per serving

These baby carrots have been boiled, then glazed with a mixture of melted butter and sugar.

The new potatoes have been roasted whole in oil, then tossed in chopped, fresh herbs.

SPICY ROAST CHICKEN

(lighter recipe)

(full recipe on page 46)

A skinless, boneless chicken breast has been lightly brushed with a mixture of lemon juice, garlic, and spices, then oven-roasted in a parchment paper parcel with no added fat.

These baby carrots have been braised in the oven in broth, dried mixed herbs, and seasoning. They are served and garnished with cumin seeds for added flavor and color.

These new potatoes have been brushed with oil, roasted, then tossed in chopped fresh herbs.

PROFITEROLES

(lighter recipe)

(full recipe on page 73)

These profiteroles have been filled with low-fat vanilla ice cream and served with a "lighter" chocolate sauce.

Serve the profiteroles with fresh, ripe strawberries and decorate with strawberry leaves or mint sprigs.

ENTRÉE: SPICY ROAST CHICKEN MEAL

(original recipe)

A boneless chicken breast with the skin left on has been brushed with olive oil flavored with lemon juice, garlic, and spices, then roasted in the oven with some butter.

Steamed broccoli is low in calories and fat, and is a good source of vitamin C.

DESSERT: PROFITEROLES

(original recipe)

These profiteroles have been filled with whipped cream and served with a rich chocolate sauce.

HOW WE REDUCED CALORIES AND FAT

- removed skin from the chicken breast
- roasted the chicken breast in a parchment paper parcel rather than roasting it with the addition of butter
- brushed the potatoes lightly with a small amount of oil rather than letting them sit in a larger amount of oil
- braised the carrots in broth and herbs, rather than glazing them in a mixture of melted butter and sugar

Calories saved = 435 calories per serving

Fat saved = 46.1 g fat per serving

- used low-fat spread in place of butter or margarine to make the choux pastry
- omitted the butter and cream traditionally added to the chocolate sauce
- reduced the quantity of chocolate used to make the chocolate sauce, and therefore slightly reduced the amount of chocolate sauce served with the profiteroles
- filled the profiteroles with reduced-fat ice cream in place of whipped cream

Calories saved = 138 calories per serving

Fat saved = 21.3 g fat per serving

TIPS FOR REDUCING FAT AND CALORIES

PREPARING FOODS

● Choose leaner cuts of meat and cut any visible fat off the meat before cooking. Buy smaller amounts of meat and replace it with vegetables, beans, or lentils.

● Try using low-fat alternatives to meat such as tofu in recipes.

● When using reduced-fat hard cheese such as Cheddar, Monterey jack, or Colby in recipes, use full-flavored varieties so that you are able to use less and retain the flavor.

● Grate or shred cheese finely rather than coarsely — the quantity will go a lot further so that you use less cheese.

● Use water from vegetables, broth cubes, and herbs to make gravies rather than using the meat juices.

● When using oil in a recipe, measure out the oil accurately using measuring spoons rather than pouring the oil straight from the bottle and guessing the amount.

● Use mashed potatoes or a mixture of cooked, mashed root vegetables such as potatoes, carrots, and rutabaga, to top savory dishes instead of pastry.

● Thicken sauces with cornstarch or arrowroot rather than using a butter and flour "roux."

● If using pastry for a pie, make a pie with one crust rather than two crusts, and use whole-wheat pastry made with poly or monounsaturated margarine.

● Use low-fat yogurt, reduced-fat mayonnaise, or low-fat curd cheese as the basis for low-fat or reduced-fat salad dressings.

● Extend reduced-fat mayonnaise with low-fat natural yogurt or curd cheese. Alternatively, thin it down using skim milk or tomato juice and add lots of fat-free or low-fat flavorings such as herbs, spices, mustard, honey, etc. for delicious low-calorie, low-fat salad dressings.

● Use tomato juice or tomato paste mixed with liquid as the basis for a salad dressing.

COOKING FOODS

● Grill, broil, poach, microwave, steam, or boil food whenever possible.

● Choose oven-baked french fries, or if making your own french fries, make thick-cut fries and fry them in unsaturated oil such as sunflower or corn oil.

● When cooking food in a wok, use only a small amount of oil or wine, fruit juice, or low-fat or fat-free broth in place of oil.

● Avoid frying foods as much as possible, but if you do fry foods, use an oil that is high in unsaturates such as sunflower, olive, or canola oil, and use as little as possible.

● "Sweat" or cook vegetables in a covered pan in their own juices, rather than frying or sautéing them, or soften in a little low-fat broth, wine, or water.

● Baste foods with fruit juice or a fat-free marinade instead of adding fat when broiling, grilling, or barbecuing.

● Roast meats on a rack so that some of the fat will drain away from the meat collected under the roast.

● When stewing tougher cuts of meat, skim off and discard any fat that rises to the surface during cooking.

● Dry-fry ground meats and other meats, and drain off excess fat before adding vegetables and other ingredients for casseroles, etc.

SERVING FOODS

● When serving cooked vegetables, toss them in chopped fresh mixed herbs and/or a splash of lemon juice for added flavor and color, rather than dotting with butter to serve.

● Garnish savory dishes with chopped fresh herbs, watercress, or a sprinkling of seeds such as cumin or sesame, to add flavor, colour, and texture to the food.

● Choose baked or boiled potatoes in place of french fries, roasted, or fried potatoes.

● Mash potatoes with skim milk or yogurt and seasoning instead of using butter and whole milk.

● Spread toasted muffins, coffeecake, and bagels with low-fat or very low-fat spread or with fat-free products such as reduced-sugar jam or jelly.

● In sandwiches, spread the bread with low-fat or fat-free dressing or mayonnaise instead of using full-fat spreads.

PREPARING AND SERVING DESSERTS

● Choose fruit canned in fruit juice rather than in syrup.

● Use skim milk to make sauces, baked desserts, scones, and batter mixtures, etc.

● Use dried or fresh fruit purées in place of all or some of the fat in suitable baking recipes (see the feature on page 68).

● Reduce the quantity of sugar in a recipe and replace it with dried fruit such as apricots or yellow raisins, or fresh fruit such as bananas.

● Decorate desserts with fresh herb sprigs such as mint sprigs, edible flowers, or slices or twists of fruit in place of piped cream or chocolate.

A small amount of fat is essential for our general health and well-being, but we can all afford to cut down on our fat intake to some extent.

It is often unnecessary to add fat to food to enhance its flavor, texture, and appearance, and there are many alternative fat-free or low-fat ingredients that can make food more palatable and appetizing just as effectively.

Such ingredients include fruit and vegetable juices, fruit and vegetable purées, wine, liquor, garlic, fresh and dried herbs and spices, edible flowers, black pepper, flavoring extracts, mustards, vinegars, fruit rinds, root ginger, tea, vegetable extract, vegetable broth, sauces such as soy sauce, pickles, and dried vegetables such as dry-packed sun-dried tomatoes.

Spices are best crushed or ground freshly at home just before using for maximum flavor and aroma, and fresh herbs are best chopped at the last minute to obtain optimum flavor and color. See the feature on page 62 for creative ideas for using herbs in low-fat cooking.

By making a few simple changes, you can create delicious recipes and meals without having to add fat. For example, a classic dish such as ratatouille — a mixture of bell pepper, zucchini, eggplant, and tomato — where traditionally you would add olive oil, tastes just as good when the oil is replaced with red or white wine.

MARINATING FOODS

Marinating foods in mixtures of wine and herbs or fruit juice and spices will help to tenderize and moisten it, as well as adding flavor and color. The marinade can then be used for basting the food as it cooks, or use it to make an accompanying sauce.

Try marinating beef and vegetable kabobs in a blend of apple juice, sherry, tomato ketchup, and other flavorings, and cook them in a microwave oven.

For an exciting low-fat dessert, bake fruit kabobs in the oven in a mixture of fruit juice and spices.

FAT-FREE COOKING METHODS

Fats are often used to cook food, to add substance and richness. Frying and roasting are two typical cooking methods that come to mind when thinking about cooking with fat. However, even these two traditionally high-fat cooking methods can be employed with little or no fat. There are many other fat-free cooking methods besides, including steaming, broiling, grilling, baking, microwaving, poaching, barbecuing, braising, and pressure-cooking. Most foods can be cooked by these fat-free methods to create delicious and nutritious meals.

QUICK TIPS FOR FAT-FREE COOKING

FRYING
● cook or "sweat" vegetables or meat in a small amount of low-fat broth, wine, or flavored water in place of oil or butter.
● use good quality nonstick cookware to prevent the food from sticking to the pan
● if you need to use some fat, use a spray oil or a mixture of oil and water in a spray bottle, to minimize the amount of fat used.
● when cooking food in a wok, use a small amount of fat-free or low-fat cooking liquid such as wine, sherry, or low-fat broth in place of oil.

ROASTING
● roast meat and poultry portions in low-fat broth, wine, or fruit juices flavored with spices and/or herbs.

DRY-ROASTING
● make your own homemade snacks by dry-roasting thin slivers of potatoes, sweet potatoes, or other vegetables.

STEAMING AND POACHING
● steam vegetables, fish, poultry, etc. with herbs or spices, and flavor the water with garlic or herbs.

BROILING, GRILLING, AND BARBECUING
● marinate the food in blends of wine, herbs, fruit juices, and other flavorings, and use the marinade to baste the food during cooking.

BAKING
● use good quality nonstick ovenware that does not require greasing before use.
● grease pans lightly with fat when necessary and then line the cake-pans with parchment or nonstick baking paper.
● line baking sheets with nonstick baking paper rather than greasing the pan.
● bake fish, poultry, etc. in foil or in parchment paper parcels with a little wine, fruit juice, or broth and flavorings.
● use low-fat spreads in place of butter or margarine in some recipes (see page 17 for more details).
● use dried fruit purées such as apricot or prune purée in place of fat in some baked cake recipes (see page 68 for more details, and page 69 for a recipe using dried fruit purée).

MICROWAVING AND PRESSURE-COOKING
● season the food and cook in small amounts of flavored low-fat broth, wine, or fruit juice.

BRAISING
● braise foods in blends of fruit juice, wine, low-fat broth, and flavorings such as spices or herbs.

FATS IN COOKING

Reduce the amount of fat used for cooking foods as much as possible and always use an oil or a soft margarine that is high in unsaturates. Avoid fats that are high in saturated fats such as butter and hard margarine, and choose a soft vegetable margarine that is high in polyunsaturated or mono-unsaturated fats. Hard margarines tend to be higher in saturated fats than soft margarines.

Choose pure vegetable oils that are low in saturates such as grapeseed, olive, sunflower, safflower, canola, soya, and corn oil rather than oils that are blended or have been hydrogenated. Sunflower oil is particularly rich in vitamin E. Some nut oils, including palm oil, coconut oil, and peanut oil, contain higher levels of saturated fats, so avoid using these too often.

LOW-FAT SPREADS

A wide range of low-fat and very low-fat spreads are widely available, and some are suitable for using in cooking as well as for spreading. Very low-fat spreads, which have a fat content of about 20%, are only suitable for spreading and are not suitable for cooking due to their high water content.

Low-fat spreads, which have a fat content of about 40%, are suitable for some cooking methods. They can be used for some all-in-one cake and cookie recipes, all-in-one sauces, choux pastry, for gently cooking or sautéing vegetables, and for some cake icings. They are not suitable for deep-fat or shallow frying, clarifying, pastry-making, some types of cookie, shortbread, rich fruit cakes, or preserves such as lemon curd or lemon cheese.

When heating low-fat spreads for a recipe, always melt the spread over a gentle heat and do not allow it to boil, since this may cause the product to spit, burn, or spoil. All-in-one sauces should be whisked continuously during cooking over a low heat. Low-fat spreads may in cooking behave slightly differently than full-fat products such as butter, but the results will be just as acceptable and you won't even notice the difference.

Some cooked products made with half or low-fat spreads may be slightly different in texture, but again they are just as delicious. For example, choux pastry made using low-fat spread may be slightly more crisp and light in texture than choux pastry made using butter or margarine. Sponge cakes tend to have a slightly lighter texture, and uncooked graham cracker cheesecake bases may not be quite so crisp. The shelf-life of cooked products made using low-fat spreads may be reduced due to the lower fat content, but you can be sure that these goodies will have gone before the food becomes stale!

NUTRITIONAL ANALYSES

Nutritional information for each recipe in the book is provided in easy-reference panels. The nutritional figures are per serving of the recipe in each case, and do not include any serving suggestions that may be included in the introduction or at the end of a recipe. These analyses have been compiled as accurately as possible, but the nutritional content of foods will vary depending on their source.

As well as specifying the number of calories per serving, the nutritional analysis also gives the overall fat content, which is then broken down into the three main types of fat: saturates, monounsaturates, and polyunsaturates.

The recommended daily intake of dietary fiber is betwen 12 and 18 g. The figures given in the nutritional analyses indicate how much fiber each recipe contributes to your daily total.

Figures for the sodium content of each recipe are also included. This figure does not include any seasoning (i.e. salt) that is added to the recipe during preparation and cooking.

The nutritional analyses detail the percentage of total calories from fat, and the percentage of calories from saturated fat is also given — in a healthy diet, this should provide no more than 10% of calories.

Where a nutritional analysis states that a recipe is a good source of a particular vitamin, mineral, or another nutrient, this indicates that a serving of the recipe will make a significant contribution to the recommended daily allowance (RDA) of the nutrients.

A GUIDE TO THE RECIPES

● All spoon measurements refer to American Standard measuring spoons, and all measurements given are for level spoons unless otherwise stated.

● The cooking times for all the recipes in this book are based on the oven or broiler being preheated.

● All eggs used in the recipes are medium (weighing 21 ounces per dozen) eggs.

KEY TO SYMBOLS

 Suitable for freezing.

 Suitable for cooking in a microwave oven.

 Suitable for vegetarians.

Please note that the term vegetarian applies to lacto-ovo vegetarians, i.e. people who eat eggs and dairy products but not meat, fish, and poultry, nor any products derived from these foods.

CHAPTER ONE

BREAKFASTS & BRUNCHES

W̲hether you're an early riser or a late sleeper, breakfast is a critical part of your day. Make your mornings both healthy and memorable with nutritious and delicious dishes. Here is a selection of quick and easy breakfast and brunch recipes, some sweetly fruity and others satisfyingly savory, but all as appetizing as they are nourishing, to ensure a positive start to your day.

BROILED FRUIT
KABOBS

Serve these delectable warm kabobs with low-fat plain or fruit-flavored yogurt for an appetizing and refreshing start to the day. Alternatively, they can be served with low-fat ice cream or reduced-fat cream for a delightful dessert.

Preparation time: 15 minutes

Cooking time: 5-10 minutes

Serves 4

2 small bananas
juice of 1 lemon
8 canned pineapple cubes in fruit juice, drained
1 pink grapefruit, peeled and segmented
8 ready-to-eat dried pitted prunes
8 ready-to-eat dried apricots
2 tbsp unsweetened orange juice
1 tbsp clear honey
¹/₂ tsp ground mixed spice

1 Peel and slice the bananas into chunks and toss them in lemon juice, to prevent browning.

2 Thread the fresh and dried fruit onto 4 long skewers, dividing the ingredients equally between the kabobs.

3 Mix together the orange juice, honey, and mixed spice, and brush over the kabobs.

4 Barbecue the kabobs or broil under a preheated broiler for 5-10 minutes, turning frequently. Brush the kabobs with any remaining orange juice mixture while they are cooking, to prevent them from drying out.

5 Serve the warm kabobs with low-fat plain yogurt.

VARIATIONS
● Use other fresh, canned, and dried fruits of your choice, such as oranges, peaches, kiwi fruits, pears, and raisins.
● Use pineapple or apple juice in place of the orange juice.
● Use ground cinnamon or nutmeg in place of the mixed spice.

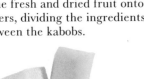

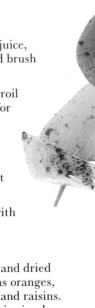

BRAN FRUIT
CEREAL

*This tasty and nutritious whole-grain
cereal mixed with fruits is ideal for breakfast
or as a filling dish for brunch.*

Preparation time: 15 minutes
Serves 6

4 tbsp rolled oats
4 tbsp bran flakes
2 tbsp wheat flakes
2 tbsp barley flakes
2 tbsp sunflower seeds
1/2 cup yellow raisins
2 tbsp dried pears, chopped
2 tbsp dried apples, chopped
2 tbsp dried peaches, chopped
2 cups small strawberries, hulled and halved
1 cup raspberries

1 Place the rolled oats, bran flakes, wheat flakes, barley flakes, sunflower seeds, and dried fruits in a large bowl and mix well. Spoon the cereal into 6 serving bowls.

2 Combine the strawberries and raspberries, and scatter them over the cereal, dividing them equally between the bowls.

3 Serve immediately with skim milk or low-fat plain yogurt.

VARIATIONS
● Use rye flakes and jumbo oats in place of the wheat flakes and rolled oats.
● Use other dried fruits such as raisins, apricots, and pineapple in place of the yellow raisins, apples, and pears.
● Use chopped nuts such as almonds, pecans, or brazil nuts in place of the sunflower seeds.
● Top the cereal with fresh fruit of your choice such as sliced kiwi fruit and peaches.

COOK'S TIP
● Make up a large batch of this whole-grain cereal and store it in an airtight container. Add the fresh fruit just before serving.

NUTRITIONAL ANALYSIS

(figures are per serving)

Calories = 136
Fat = 0.4g
of which saturates = 0.04g
      monounsaturates = 0g
      polyunsaturates = 0.04g
Protein = 2.2g
Carbohydrate = 33.0g
Dietary fiber = 3.5g
Sodium = 0g

Percentage of total calories from fat = 3%
of which saturates = 0.3%
Good source of vitamin C

NUTRITIONAL ANALYSIS

(figures are per serving)

Calories = 217
Fat = 4.2g
of which saturates = 0.6g
      monounsaturates = 0.5g
      polyunsaturates = 1.8g

Protein = 6.5g
Carbohydrate = 40.0g
Dietary fiber = 7.4g
Sodium = 0.01g

Percentage of total calories from fat = 17%, of which saturates = 2%

SAVORY
RICE

Smoked fish and rice are a delicious combination, and ensure an energy-packed start to the day.

Preparation time: 15 minutes

Cooking time: 40 minutes

Serves 4

*³/₄ cup long-grain brown rice
12 ounces skinless, smoked fish fillets, such as finnan haddie, smoked cod, or smoked white fish
1 small onion, minced
¹/₂ cup button mushrooms, sliced
2 eggs, hard-boiled
3 tbsp low-fat or 2% milk
2 tbsp minced fresh parsley
salt and freshly ground black pepper
juice of 1 lime (optional)
fresh lime slices and fresh herb sprigs, to garnish*

1 Cook the rice in a saucepan of lightly salted, boiling water for about 30-35 minutes, until just cooked and tender. Drain thoroughly and keep hot.

2 Meanwhile, place the fish fillets, onion, and mushrooms in a large nonstick skillet with a lid, and cover with water. Cover, bring to the boil, and simmer gently for 10-15 minutes, until the fish is just cooked and tender.

3 Drain, reserving the fish, onion, and mushrooms and discarding the remaining liquid. Flake the fish and set aside. Peel the eggs, discard the shells, and chop the eggs coarsely.

4 Place the milk in a nonstick saucepan. Add the cooked rice, fish, vegetables, eggs, parsley, and seasoning and stir to mix.

5 Cook gently, stirring frequently, for about 5 minutes, until piping hot. Sprinkle with the lime juice, if using, and stir to mix.

6 Garnish with lime slices and fresh herb sprigs and serve on its own or with some fresh crusty bread.

NUTRITIONAL ANALYSIS

(figures are per serving)

Calories = 297
Fat = 5.3g
of which saturates = 1.5g
    monounsaturates = 1.8g
    polyunsaturates = 1.1g

Protein = 24.4g
Carbohydrate = 40.5 g
Dietary fiber = 1.6g
Sodium = 0.7g

Percentage of total calories from fat = 16%
of which saturates = 5%
Good source of vitamin B12

VARIATIONS
● Use smoked oysters or marinated salmon in place of smoked white fish.
● Use lemon juice in place of the lime juice.
● Use long-grain white rice in place of the brown rice.

COOK'S TIP
● Reserve the fish cooking liquid and use as broth for another recipe. Freeze for later use when it has cooled.

SAUTÉED POTATOES WITH
BACON & HERBS

*This recipe makes a great start to the day.
Serve it with toast for breakfast or with poached eggs for
a more substantial brunch.*

Preparation time: 10 minutes

Cooking time: 15-20 minutes

Serves 4

2 tsp sunflower oil
1 pound (4 cups) boiled potatoes, cooled and diced
4 shallots, minced
4 slices smoked lean bacon, trimmed and diced
2-3 tbsp chopped fresh mixed herbs or
1-2 tsp dried herbs
salt and freshly ground black pepper

1 Heat the oil in a nonstick skillet and add the potatoes, shallots, and bacon.

2 Cook over a medium heat, stirring frequently, until the potatoes are browned and the bacon is cooked.

3 Add the herbs and seasoning, mix well, and serve immediately with fresh crusty bread or toast.

NUTRITIONAL ANALYSIS
(figures are per serving)

Calories = 129
Fat = 3.1g
of which saturates = 0.8g
monounsaturates = 1.7g
polyunsaturates = 0.4g

Protein = 6.4g
Carbohydrate = 20.0g
Dietary fiber = 1.7g
Sodium = 0.4g

Percentage of total calories from fat = 22%, of which saturates = 5%

APPLE & CINNAMON
COFFEECAKE

Serve this deliciously moist, yeastless coffeecake warm or cold, on its own or with a thin scraping of low-fat spread or reduced-sugar jam or jelly.

Preparation time: 20 minutes
Cooking time: 25-30 minutes
Makes 8 wedges

1 cup self-rising flour
1 cup whole-wheat flour
¹/₂ tsp double-acting baking powder
pinch of salt
1 tsp baking soda
4 tbsp soft margarine
4 tbsp light soft brown sugar
1 tsp ground cinnamon
1 medium-size tart apple, peeled,
cored, and coarsely grated
3-4 tbsp skim milk,
plus extra for glazing
1 tbsp light brown sugar

1 Sieve the flours, baking powder, salt, and baking soda into a bowl. Rub in the margarine until the mixture resembles bread crumbs.

2 Stir in the soft brown sugar and cinnamon, then add the grated apples and mix well. Stir in enough milk to give a soft but not sticky dough.

3 Turn the dough onto a floured surface, knead lightly, and form into a 7-inch round.

4 Place the cake on a lightly floured cookie sheet, brush the top with milk, and sprinkle with the light brown sugar. Mark the cake into 8 even wedges.

5 Bake in a preheated oven at 400° for 25-30 minutes, until risen and golden brown.

6 Transfer to a wire rack to cool and break into wedges to serve. Serve warm or cold on its own, or with a thin scraping of low-fat spread or reduced-sugar jam or jelly.

VARIATIONS
- Use all whole-wheat flour, graham flour, or all white flour in place of a mixture.
- Replace the cinnamon with ground mixed spice.
- Use white or golden granulated sugar in place of the soft brown sugar.

COOK'S TIP
- When making this kind of yeastless dough and mixing the ingredients together, never over-mix or knead the mixture too heavily, since this may result in a heavy, uneven cake.

NUTRITIONAL ANALYSIS

(figures are per wedge)

Calories = 190
Fat = 6.2g
of which saturates = 1.3g
      monounsaturates = 1.9g
      polyunsaturates = 2.7g
Protein = 3.5g
Carbohydrate = 32.5g
Dietary fiber = 2.2g
Sodium = 0.2g

Percentage of total calories from fat = 29%
of which saturates = 6%

 APRICOT & DATE
BREAKFAST LOAF

This tasty treat is an excellent choice for breakfast or brunch, and also makes a great snack for any time of the day.

Preparation time: 15 minutes, plus soaking time for the fruits

Cooking time: 1 hour

Makes one 2-pound loaf (12 slices)

1 cup ready-to-eat dried apricots, chopped
1 cup dried pitted dates, chopped
1/2 cup yellow raisins
1/2 cup light soft brown sugar
2/3 cup cold tea
2 eggs, beaten
2 cups whole-wheat flour
1 tsp baking powder
2 tsp ground mixed spice

1 Place the fruit and sugar in a bowl and stir to mix. Add the tea and mix well. Cover and leave to soak for at least 4 hours or overnight, until most of the tea has been absorbed and the fruit is plumped up.

2 Stir in the eggs, then add the flour, baking powder, and mixed spice, and mix thoroughly.

3 Turn the mixture into a lightly greased 2-pound loaf pan and level the surface.

4 Bake in a preheated oven at 350° for about 1 hour, or until firm to the touch. Cool in the pan for a few minutes, then unmold onto a wire rack to cool completely.

5 Serve warm or cold in slices, on its own or with a thin scraping of low-fat spread or reduced-sugar jam or jelly.

VARIATIONS
- Use a mixture of dried fruits of your choice such as papaya and raisins.
- Use ground cinnamon in place of the mixed spice.

NUTRITIONAL ANALYSIS

(figures are per slice)

Calories = 196
Fat = 1.6g
of which saturates = 0.4g
      monounsaturates = 0.5g
      polyunsaturates = 0.3g
Protein = 4.9g
Carbohydrate = 43.6g
Dietary fiber = 3.4g
Sodium = 0.02g

Percentage of total calories from fat = 7%
of which saturates = 2%

CHAPTER TWO

SOUPS & APPETIZERS

*I*n taking the time and effort to make your own soups, you will be rewarded both
by quality flavor and a high level of nutrients. Here are hearty hot soups as
well as refreshing chilled soups, all of which are quick and easy to prepare.
Your choice of appetizer should relate to the composition of the meal as a whole.
A good appetizer will complement rather than copy the taste and appearance
of the entrée. Choose accordingly from this delicious selection, ranging from
dips and cocktails to classics such as Macaroni and Cheese.

FRESH TOMATO & BASIL SOUP

*This is a light, fresh-tasting soup ideal served with thick slices of fresh
crusty bread or bread rolls.*

Preparation time: 15 minutes
Cooking time: 30 minutes
Serves 4

2 pounds tomatoes, roughly chopped
2 onions, chopped
8 ounces carrots, sliced
3³/₄ cups vegetable broth
1 tbsp tomato paste
pinch of sugar
salt and freshly ground black pepper
3 tbsp chopped fresh basil

1 Place all the ingredients,
except the basil, in a large
saucepan and mix well.

2 Cover, bring to the boil, and
simmer for about 30 minutes,
stirring occasionally, until the
vegetables are tender.

3 Cool the mixture slightly, then
transfer it to a blender or food
processor and blend until smooth.

4 Strain the soup through a sieve and
discard the pulp.

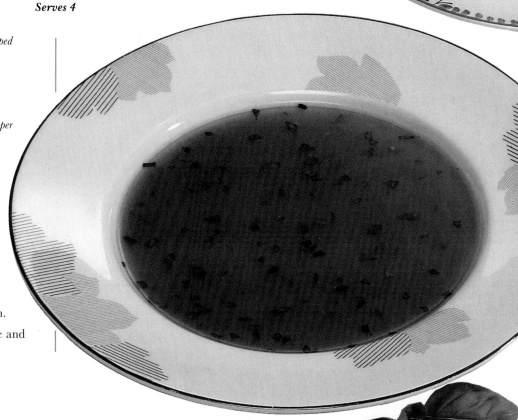

5 Return the mixture to the saucepan and stir in the basil. Reheat gently and adjust the seasoning before serving. Serve with fresh crusty bread rolls.

VARIATIONS
● Use other chopped fresh herbs such as coriander (cilantro), parsley, or mixed fresh herbs in place of the basil.
● Use two 14-ounce cans chopped tomatoes in place of the fresh tomatoes.
● Use 2 trimmed and sliced leeks in place of the onions.

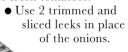

Try creating your own delicious light soups with other simple mixtures of vegetables such as leek and potato, carrot and coriander (cilantro), cauliflower and broccoli (flavored with chili powder), spinach and nutmeg, tomato, lentil, and onion, watercress and onion, or celery and parsley.

NUTRITIONAL ANALYSIS
(figures are per serving)

Calories = 98
Fat = 1.5g
of which saturates = 0.3g
    monounsaturates = 0.2g
    polyunsaturates = 0.6g
Protein = 3.4g
Carbohydrate = 18.8g
Dietary fiber = 4.8g
Sodium = 0.5g

Percentage of total calories from fat = 14%
of which saturates = 3%
Good source of vitamins A, C, & E

CHILLED CUCUMBER & MINT SOUP

An elegant, refreshing soup that would bring a cooling note to a balmy summer evening.

Preparation time: 15 minutes, plus 20 minutes standing time for the cucumber, plus chilling time
Serves 4

2 cucumbers, peeled and cut into large cubes
1 small onion, chopped
1 clove garlic, crushed
2 cups low-fat plain yogurt
²/₃ cup vegetable broth, cooled
2 tbsp chopped fresh mint
salt and freshly ground black pepper
fresh mint sprigs, to garnish

1 Place the cucumber in a bowl, sprinkle with salt, and set aside for 20 minutes. Rinse thoroughly and pat dry with paper towels.

2 Place the cucumber, onion, garlic, yogurt, broth, mint, and seasoning in a blender or food processor and blend until relatively smooth and well mixed. Taste and add more seasoning, if needed.

3 Pour into a bowl, cover, and chill before serving. Garnish with fresh mint sprigs and serve with thick slices of fresh whole-wheat bread or toast.

VARIATIONS
● Use other herbs such as tarragon, parsley, coriander (cilantro), or mixed herbs in place of the mint.
● Use 4 shallots in place of the onion.

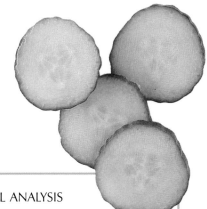

NUTRITIONAL ANALYSIS
(figures are per serving)

Calories = 89
Fat = 1.3g
of which saturates = 0.6g
    monounsaturates = 0.2g
    polyunsaturates = 0g

Protein = 7.4g
Carbohydrate = 12.3g
Dietary fiber = 0.9g
Sodium = 0.2g

Percentage of total calories from fat = 13%, of which saturates = 6%

MACARONI
& CHEESE

This is a light version of the popular dish, lower in fat and calories than the traditional recipe. Serve as an appetizer or as a filling snack at lunctime.

Preparation time: 25 minutes

Cooking time: 30 minutes

Serves 6

7 ounces whole-wheat macaroni
2 leeks, washed, trimmed, and sliced
3 tbsp vegetable broth
2 tbsp low-fat spread (suitable for cooking)
2 tbsp all-purpose flour
2¹/₂ cups skim milk
¹/₂ tsp prepared mustard (American-style or English-style)
salt and freshly ground black pepper
¹/₂ cup finely grated reduced-fat mature Cheddar cheese
2 tbsp whole-wheat bread crumbs
1-2 tbsp chopped fresh chives
fresh chives, to garnish

1 Cook the macaroni in a saucepan of lightly salted, boiling water for 10 minutes, until just tender. Drain thoroughly and keep warm.

2 Meanwhile, place the leeks and broth in a saucepan, cover, and cook gently for about 10 minutes, stirring occasionally, until the leeks are just tender. Drain thoroughly.

3 Place the low-fat spread, flour, and milk in a saucepan and heat gently, whisking continuously, until the sauce comes to the boil and thickens. Simmer gently for 3 minutes, whisking.

4 Remove the pan from the heat, add the mustard, seasoning, and 6 tbsp of the grated cheese and stir until the cheese has melted.

5 Add the macaroni and leeks, mix well, and transfer to an ovenproof dish. Mix together the remaining cheese, bread crumbs, and chives and sprinkle evenly over the top.

6 Bake in a preheated oven at 375° for about 30 minutes, until golden brown and bubbling.

7 Garnish with chives and serve with fresh crusty bread or slices of tomato.

VARIATIONS
● Use white macaroni in place of the whole-wheat macaroni.
● Use 1 large onion in place of the leeks.
● Use fresh parsley in place of the chives.
● Use white bread crumbs in place of the whole-wheat bread crumbs.

NUTRITIONAL ANALYSIS

(figures are per serving)

Calories = 219
Fat = 5.6g
of which saturates = 2.5g
      monounsaturates = 1.0g
      polyunsaturates = 0.9g
Protein = 14.1g
Carbohydrate = 29.8g
Dietary fiber = 2.2g
Sodium = 0.2g

Percentage of total calories from fat = 23%
of which saturates = 10%

SPICY PUMPKIN
SOUP

A warming winter soup, full of subtle spice and flavor.
Serve as an appetizer before a light entrée or as a filling snack.

Preparation time: 15 minutes
Cooking time: 20-25 minutes
Serves 4

1 tsp olive oil
2 onions, sliced
1 clove garlic, crushed
1 tsp ground cumin
1 tsp ground coriander (cilantro)
1 tsp chili powder
2 cups skim milk
2 cups vegetable broth
salt and freshly ground black pepper
fresh coriander (cilantro) leaves, to garnish

1 Remove and discard the skin and seeds from the pumpkin and dice the flesh. Set aside while the onions are being cooked.

2 Heat the oil in a large saucepan and gently cook the onions and garlic for 5 minutes, stirring occasionally.

3 Add the diced pumpkin and spices and cook for 5 minutes, stirring occasionally.

4 Stir in the milk, broth, and seasoning and mix well. Cover, bring to the boil, and simmer gently for 15-20 minutes, stirring occasionally, until the pumpkin is cooked and tender.

5 Allow the mixture to cool slightly, then place in a blender or food processor and blend until smooth.

6 Return the soup to the saucepan, adjust the seasoning, and reheat gently before serving.

7 Garnish with fresh coriander (cilantro) leaves and serve with crusty French bread.

VARIATIONS
● Use winter squash in place of the pumpkin.
● Use 3 trimmed and sliced leeks in place of the onions.
● Use your own choice of ground mixed spices or chopped fresh herbs.

NUTRITIONAL ANALYSIS
(figures are per serving)

Calories = 105
Fat = 1.9g
of which saturates = 0.4g
      monounsaturates = 0.5g
      polyunsaturates = 0.1g

Protein = 6.7g
Carbohydrate = 16.9g
Dietary fiber = 3.3g
Sodium = 0.3g

Percentage of total calories from fat − 17%, of which saturates = 4%

HERBED MUSHROOM
PÂTÉ

*A light pâté that is excellent spread on thick slices
of toast or fresh bread for an appetizer.*

Preparation time: 30 minutes, plus cooling and chilling time

Cooking time: 1 hour

Serves 8

4 tbsp vegetable broth
1 onion, minced
2 cloves garlic, crushed
2 sticks celery, chopped
12 ounces (about 2 cups) closed cup mushrooms,
sliced
12 ounces (about 2 cups) brown cap mushrooms,
sliced
3-4 tbsp chopped fresh mixed herbs
3 tbsp port wine
salt and freshly ground black pepper
6 tbsp fresh whole-wheat bread crumbs
2 eggs, beaten
fresh herb sprigs and tomato slices, to garnish

1 Place the broth, onion, garlic, and celery
in a saucepan, cover, and cook gently for
10 minutes, stirring occasionally.

2 Stir in the mushrooms, cover, and cook
gently for 10 minutes, stirring occasionally.

3 Remove the pan from the heat, add
the herbs, port wine, and seasoning and
mix well.

4 Set aside to cool slightly, then place
the mixture in a liquidizer or food
processor and blend until smooth.
Transfer the mixture to a bowl, add the
bread crumbs and eggs, and mix well.

5 Adjust the seasoning, transfer to a
lightly greased and lined 2-pound loaf
pan, and level the surface.

6 Bake in a preheated oven at 350° for
about 1 hour, until lightly browned and
set on top.

7 Set aside to cool completely in the pan.
Once cool, cover and refrigerate for
several hours before serving.

8 To serve, turn carefully out of the pan
and garnish with fresh herb sprigs and
tomato slices. Serve in slices with fresh
crusty bread or toast.

VARIATIONS
● Use fresh parsley in place of the fresh
mixed herbs.
● Use sherry or brandy in place of the
port wine.
● Use white or brown bread crumbs in
place of the whole-wheat bread crumbs
● Use 2 leeks in place of the onion.
● Use button mushrooms in place of the
closed cap mushrooms.

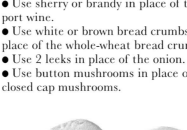

NUTRITIONAL ANALYSIS

(figures are per serving)

Calories = 72
Fat = 2.3g
of which saturates = 0.6g
      monounsaturates = 0.7g
      polyunsaturates = 0.5g
Protein = 4.7g
Carbohydrate = 7.0g
Dietary fiber = 2.0g
Sodium = 0.1g

Percentage of total calories from fat = 29%
of which saturates = 7%

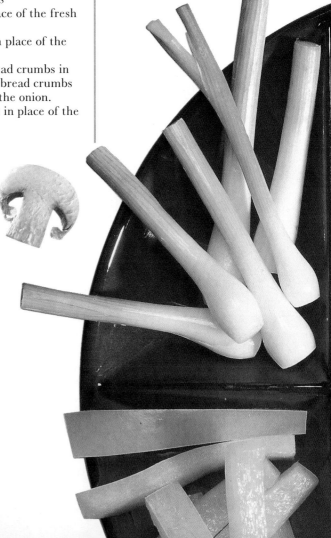

TUNA & WATERCRESS
DIP

This is a delicious and refreshing dip that is best served with a good selection of nutritious and colorful raw vegetables.

Preparation time: 10 minutes, plus chilling time

Serves 8

14-ounce can tuna in water, drained and flaked
1 pound canned pinto beans, rinsed and drained
1 cup small-curd cottage cheese
small bunch watercress, roughly chopped
2 tbsp reduced-calorie mayonnaise
2 tbsp low-fat plain yogurt
finely grated rind of 1 lime
salt and freshly ground black pepper

1 Place the tuna, beans, cottage cheese, watercress, mayonnaise, yogurt, lime rind, and seasoning in a liquidizer or food processor. Blend until the mixture is smooth and thoroughly mixed.

2 Transfer the tuna mixture to a serving dish, cover, and chill before serving.

3 Serve the dip with a selection of raw vegetables such as sticks of bell pepper, cucumber, and carrots, green onions (scallions), and baby corn cobs.

VARIATIONS

● Use canned or barbecued salmon in place of the tuna.
● Add 1-2 tbsp chopped fresh mixed herbs or fresh parsley to the mixture before serving.
● Add 1 small onion or 4 green onions (scallions), the green parts included, to the mixture before blending.

NUTRITIONAL ANALYSIS

(figures are per serving)

Calories = 112
Fat = 2.8g
of which saturates = 0.8g
     monounsaturates = 0.4g
     polyunsaturates = 0.2g
Protein = 15.6g
Carbohydrate = 6.6g
Dietary fiber = 2.0g
Sodium = 0.4g

Percentage of total calories from fat = 23%
of which saturates = 6%
Good source of vitamins B12 & D

SEAFOOD
COCKTAIL

*This combination of mixed seafood
and fresh salad ingredients, tossed
together in a tangy horseradish
dressing, makes a sumptuous
appetizer for a special occasion meal.*

Preparation time: 15 minutes
Serves 6

4 tbsp reduced-calorie mayonnaise
2 tbsp low-fat plain yogurt
2 tbsp hot horseradish sauce or grated fresh
horseradish
salt and freshly ground black pepper
2 tbsp chopped fresh mixed herbs (optional)
$1/2$ cup cooked, peeled jumbo shrimp
1 cup cooked, shelled mussels
1 cup cooked, shelled scallops
1 cup cherry (salad) tomatoes, halved
$1/2$ cucumber, diced
1 bunch green onions (scallions), chopped
mixed green salad leaves
fresh herb sprigs, to garnish

1 To make the dressing, place the
mayonnaise, yogurt, horseradish sauce,
seasoning, and herbs, if using, in a bowl
and mix together thoroughly. Set aside.

2 Place the shrimp, mussels, and scallops
in a bowl, add the tomatoes, cucumber,
and green onions (scallions) and stir to
mix. Add the dressing and toss together.

3 Arrange a bed of green salad leaves in
4 serving dishes and spoon the seafood
mixture over the top.

4 Garnish with fresh herb sprigs and
serve immediately with warm bread rolls.

VARIATIONS
● Use your own choice of cooked seafood
for this recipe.
● Use salad ingredients of your choice
such as radishes, sugar-snap peas,
and mushrooms.
● Use whole-grain mustard in place
of the horseradish.

NUTRITIONAL ANALYSIS
(figures are per serving)

Calories = 144	Protein = 19.4g
Fat = 4.9g	Carbohydrate = 3.9g
of which saturates = 0.8g	Dietary fiber = 0.8g
monounsaturates = 1.0g	Sodium = 0.8g
polyunsaturates = 2.5g	

Percentage of total calories from fat = 31%, of which saturates = 5%
Good source of vitamin B12

AVOCADO & SHRIMP
COCKTAIL

*In this light version of an old favorite, diced avocado
and plump shrimp are brought together in a tasty yogurt dressing.*

Preparation time: 15 minutes
Serves 4

FOR THE DRESSING
*2/3 cup low-fat plain yogurt
1 tsp honey
1 tbsp tomato ketchup
1 tbsp chopped fresh coriander (cilantro)
dash of Tabasco sauce
salt and freshly ground black pepper*

FOR THE COCKTAIL
*1 small avocado
lemon juice, for sprinkling
4 green onions (scallions), chopped
1/2 cucumber, peeled and sliced
1 small green bell pepper, seeded and diced
8 cooked jumbo shrimp
shredded lettuce
fresh coriander (cilantro) leaves, to garnish*

1 Place all the dressing ingredients in
a bowl and mix well. Set aside.

2 Peel, pit, and dice the avocado and
sprinkle with lemon juice to prevent
discoloration.

3 Place the diced avocado, green onions
(scallions), cucumber, bell pepper, and
shrimp in a bowl and stir to mix.

4 Arrange a bed of shredded lettuce in
4 serving dishes. Top with the avocado-
and-shrimp mixture.

5 Spoon some dressing over each
portion, garnish with fresh coriander
(cilantro) leaves, and serve
immediately with thick slices of fresh
crusty whole-wheat bread.

VARIATIONS
● Add 1 tsp chili powder, ground
coriander (cilantro), or cumin to the
mayonnaise mixture.
● Use cooked, shelled clams, scallops,
or mussels in place of the shrimp.
● Add 1 crushed clove of garlic
to the dressing for added piquancy,
if preferred.

NUTRITIONAL ANALYSIS

(figures are per serving)

Calories = 151
Fat = 6.0g
of which saturates = 1.4g
    monounsaturates = 3.2g
    polyunsaturates = 0.8g
Protein = 17.3g
Carbohydrate = 7.3g
Dietary fiber = 1.5g
Sodium = 1.1g

Percentage of total calories from fat = 35%
of which saturates = 8%
Good source of vitamin B12

PEARS WITH
BLUE CHEESE

*A creamy blue cheese sauce
complements perfectly the luscious
fruity flavor of pears in this dish.
Try serving the sauce as a baked
potato topping for a delicious entrée.*

Preparation time: 15 minutes
Serves 6

*1/2 cup low-fat soft cheese with garlic and herbs
1/3 cup whole milk plain yogurt
2 tbsp crumbled mature blue cheese
6 large ripe pears
juice of 1 lemon*

1 Place the soft cheese, yogurt, and blue
cheese in a small bowl and blend
together until smooth and well mixed.

2 Peel, core, and slice the pears and toss
them in lemon juice.

3 Arrange the pear slices on serving
plates and spoon the blue cheese sauce
alongside the pears. Serve immediately.

VARIATION
● Any variety of strongly flavored soft
cheese, such as Stilton or Gorgonzola,
can be used for the sauce.

NUTRITIONAL ANALYSIS

(figures are per serving)

Calories = 155
Fat = 4.3g
of which saturates = 1.8g
    monounsaturates = 0.9g
    polyunsaturates = 0.1g
Protein = 6.0g
Carbohydrate = 24.5g
Dietary fiber = 3.7g
Sodium = 0.1g

Percentage of total calories from fat = 25%
of which saturates = 10%

CHAPTER THREE

LIGHT DISHES & SNACKS

Be it lunchtime or dinner, eating alone or feasting with friends, this selection of delicious light dishes and snacks will impress your tastebuds every time. Try the tempting Spiced Chicken and Pepper Rolls or the filling and nutritious Roast Pepper and Mushroom Pizza, and don't miss an old favorite, Chili con Carne. They are all light choices, whether vegetarian or otherwise, full of flavor and nutrients, and are sure to satisfy even the most persistent hunger pangs.

TUNA & ZUCCHINI
OMELET

The addition of potatoes to this omelet recipe makes the dish more filling without piling on the fat or calories.

Preparation time: 20 minutes

Cooking time: 20 minutes

Serves 4

1 tsp sunflower oil
1 onion, minced
1 clove garlic, crushed
3 zucchini, thinly sliced
1 cup diced, boiled potatoes
3 eggs, plus 2 egg whites
7-ounce can tuna in water, drained and flaked
1 tbsp chopped fresh tarragon
salt and freshly ground black pepper
3 tbsp finely grated reduced-fat sharp cheese
fresh herb sprigs, to garnish

1 Heat the oil in a large nonstick skillet. Add the onion, garlic, and zucchini and cook for 5 minutes, stirring.

2 Add the potatoes and cook for 2-3 minutes, stirring.

3 Beat the eggs, egg whites, and 2 tbsp water together. Add the tuna, tarragon, and seasoning, and mix well.

4 Pour the egg mixture into the skillet and cook over a medium heat until the eggs are beginning to set and the omelet is golden brown underneath.

5 Sprinkle the cheese over the top of the tortilla and place under a preheated medium broiler. Cook until the cheese has melted and the top is golden brown.

6 Garnish with fresh herb sprigs and serve in wedges with a crisp mixed side salad.

VARIATIONS
● Use other vegetables such as blanched broccoli flowerets or peas in place of the zucchini.
● Use other fish canned in water such as salmon in place of the tuna.

SPICED
CHICKEN & PEPPER ROLLS

These flavorsome filled soft rolls make an excellent lunchtime snack or a quick and easy light supper. Try serving the spiced chicken in warmed pita pockets for a change.

Preparation time: 10 minutes

Cooking time: 6 minutes

Serves 4

1 tbsp dry sherry
1 tbsp light soy sauce
1 tsp paprika
¹/₂ tsp ground cumin
¹/₂ tsp ground coriander (cilantro)
¹/₂ tsp chili powder
salt and freshly ground black pepper
2 tsp sunflower oil
1 clove garlic, crushed
*1-inch piece fresh root ginger, peeled,
grated, or minced*
1 bunch green onions (scallions), chopped
*12 ounces skinless, boneless chicken breast, cut
into thin strips*
1 red bell pepper, seeded and diced
4 whole-wheat soft rolls
very low-fat spread, for spreading

1 Place the sherry, soy sauce, spices, and seasoning in a bowl and mix well. Set aside.

2 Heat the oil in a large nonstick skillet or wok. Add the garlic, ginger, and green onions (scallions) and stir-fry over a high heat for 30 seconds.

3 Add the chicken and stir-fry for 2 minutes. Add the bell pepper and stir fry for a further 2 minutes. Add the sherry mixture and stir-fry for 1 minute.

4 Split the rolls in half and spread each with a thin scraping of low-fat spread. Spoon some spicy chicken into each one. Top with tomato and cucumber slices, season, and serve immediately with a green side salad or low-calorie coleslaw.

VARIATION
● Experiment with different types of whole-grain bread rolls.

NUTRITIONAL ANALYSIS

(figures are per serving)

Calories = 210
Fat = 7.5g
of which saturates = 2.5g
    monounsaturates = 3.0g
    polyunsaturates = 0.9g
Protein = 23.3g
Carbohydrate = 13.3g
Dietary fiber = 1.6g
Sodium = 0.3g

Percentage of total calories from fat = 32%
of which saturates = 10%
Good source of vitamin B12

NUTRITIONAL ANALYSIS

(figures are per filled roll)

Calories = 372
Fat = 6.7g
of which saturates = 1.5g
    monounsaturates = 2.6g
    polyunsaturates = 1.5g

Protein = 32.4g
Carbohydrate = 47.5g
Dietary fiber = 7.3g
Sodium = 1.0g

Percentage of total calories from fat = 16%, of which saturates = 4%
Good source of vitamin C

CHILI CON CARNE

*A lighter version of a popular favorite,
this chili recipe is full of flavor and ideal served with boiled
brown rice or as a baked potato topping.*

Preparation time: 10 minutes

Cooking time: 1 hour, 5 minutes

Serves 4

10 ounces (1¹/₄ cups) extra-lean ground beef
2 onions, minced
1 clove garlic, crushed
2 fresh red chilies, seeded and finely chopped
1 tbsp all-purpose flour
1 tsp ground cumin
1 tsp ground coriander (cilantro)
2 tbsp tomato paste
14-ounce can peeled, chopped tomatoes
1¹/₄ cups beef broth
salt and freshly ground black pepper
14-ounce can red kidney beans, rinsed and
drained
1 large red bell pepper, seeded and diced
1¹/₄ cups sliced mushrooms

1 Place the ground beef, onions, garlic, and chilies in a large, nonstick saucepan, and cook gently until browned all over, stirring frequently.

2 Add the flour, spices, tomato paste, tomatoes, broth, and seasoning and mix.

3 Bring to the boil, stirring, then cover and simmer for 30 minutes, stirring occasionally.

4 Add the kidney beans, bell pepper, and mushrooms, and stir to mix. Cover and simmer for a further 30 minutes, stirring occasionally.

5 Serve with boiled brown rice.

VARIATIONS

● Use other lean ground meats such as pork, lamb, turkey, or chicken in place of the beef. For a vegetarian option, use ground soya.
● Use other canned beans such as pinto beans or chick-peas (garbanzo beans) in place of the kidney beans.
● Use 1-2 tsp hot chili powder in place of the fresh chilies.

NUTRITIONAL ANALYSIS

(figures are per serving)

Calories = 283
Fat = 8.1g
of which saturates = 3.1g
      monounsaturates = 2.9g
      polyunsaturates = 0.9g
Protein = 25.0g
Carbohydrate = 29.9g
Dietary fiber = 8.1g
Sodium = 0.6g

Percentage of total calories from fat = 26%
of which saturates = 10%
Good source of vitamins A, C, & B vitamins

ZUCCHINI, CHEESE, & ONION
POTATO BAKE

A scrumptious combination of potatoes, zucchini, and onions in a creamy cheese sauce makes a healthy but satisfying choice for a family meal.

Preparation time: 20 minutes

Cooking time: 1½-2 hours

Serves 6

2 tbsp low-fat spread (suitable for cooking)
2 tbsp all-purpose flour
2½ cups skim milk
½ cup finely grated reduced-fat mature yellow cheese
salt and freshly ground black pepper
1½ cups sliced zucchini
2 onions, sliced
3 tbsp chopped fresh chives
3 tbsp chopped fresh parsley
1¾ pounds potatoes, washed and thinly sliced
fresh parsley sprigs, to garnish

1 Place the low-fat spread, flour, and milk in a saucepan and heat gently, whisking continuously, until the sauce comes to the boil and thickens. Simmer gently for 3 minutes, stirring.

2 Remove the pan from the heat, add the cheese and seasoning, and stir until the cheese has melted.

3 Mix together the zucchini, onions, herbs, and seasoning.

4 Spread a layer of the zucchini mixture over the base of a lightly greased ovenproof casserole dish. Top with some potato slices. Continue layering the vegetables, ending with a layer of potatoes.

5 Pour the cheese sauce over the vegetables and cover the dish with foil.

6 Bake in a preheated oven at 350° for 1½-2 hours, until the vegetables are cooked and tender. Remove the foil for the last 30 minutes of the cooking time, to brown the potato topping.

7 Garnish with fresh parsley sprigs and serve on its own or with steamed fresh seasonal vegetables such as green beans and baby carrots. For a more substantial meal, serve with broiled fish such as cod or red snapper, and seasonal fresh vegetables.

VARIATIONS
● Use sweet potatoes or a mixture of sweet and standard potatoes.
● Use chopped fresh mixed herbs in place of the chives and parsley.

NUTRITIONAL ANALYSIS
(figures are per serving)

Calories = 231
Fat = 5.3g
of which saturates = 2.4g
    monounsaturates = 0.9g
    polyunsaturates = 0.9g

Protein = 14.3g
Carbohydrate = 33.6g
Dietary fiber = 2.9g
Sodium = 0.2g

Percentage of total calories from fat = 21%, of which saturates = 9%

SPICY SEAFOOD
PIZZA

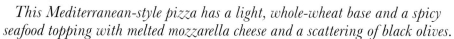

This Mediterranean-style pizza has a light, whole-wheat base and a spicy seafood topping with melted mozzarella cheese and a scattering of black olives.

Preparation time: 30 minutes, plus kneading and rising time for the pizza dough

Cooking time: 25-35 minutes

Serves 6

1 recipe pizza dough (see opposite)
1 tsp olive oil
1 red onion, sliced
1 yellow bell pepper, seeded and diced
1 clove garlic, crushed
1 recipe tomato sauce (see opposite)
1¹/₂ cups shelled mixed seafood
1 tsp ground coriander (cilantro)
1 tsp ground cumin
1 tsp chili powder
1 tsp ground ginger
¹/₃ cup shredded mozzarella cheese
16 black olives
fresh herb sprigs, to garnish

1 Prepare and shape the pizza dough as instructed opposite.

2 Heat the oil in a saucepan, add the onion, bell pepper, and garlic and cook gently for 5-10 minutes, stirring occasionally, until the vegetables begin to soften.

3 Spread the tomato sauce evenly over the pizza base, then the onion mixture.

4 Place the seafood and spices in a bowl and mix well. Spoon over the pizza.

5 Sprinkle the cheese over the pizza and scatter the olives over the top.

6 Bake in a preheated oven at 425°, for 25-35 minutes, until the dough is risen and the pizza is golden brown.

7 Garnish with fresh herb sprigs and serve hot or cold in slices with a tossed green salad or homemade low-calorie coleslaw.

VARIATIONS
● Use a flavored oil such as chili or herb oil in place of the olive oil.
● Use jumbo shrimp in place of the mixed seafood.
● Use reduced-fat yellow cheese such as Cheddar in place of the mozzarella.

NUTRITIONAL ANALYSIS

(figures are per serving)

Calories = 294

Fat = 8.3g

of which   saturates = 2.6g

monounsaturates = 3.3g

polyunsaturates = 1.0g

Protein = 22.7g

Carbohydrate = 34.0g

Dietary fiber = 4.0g

Sodium = 1.0g

Percentage of calories from fat = 25%, of which saturates = 8%

Good source of vitamins B12 & C

TOMATO SAUCE

14-ounce can peeled, chopped tomatoes
1 small onion, minced
1 clove garlic, crushed
1 tbsp tomato paste
1 tbsp chopped fresh mixed herbs
or 1 tsp dried herbs
pinch of sugar
salt and freshly ground black pepper

Place all the ingredients
in a saucepan. Bring to
the boil, then simmer,
uncovered, for 15-20
minutes, until the
sauce becomes fairly
thick. Adjust the
seasoning and use
as a base topping
for your pizza.

BASIC PIZZA DOUGH

$1/_2$ oz fresh yeast or 1 package active dry yeast
$1/_2$ tsp sugar
$2/_3$ cup warm water
1 cup all-purpose flour
1 cup whole-wheat flour
$1/_2$ tsp salt
1 tbsp olive oil

1 Blend the fresh yeast with the sugar
and water and set aside until frothy.
For dried yeast, mix the sugar with
the water, sprinkle the yeast over the
water, then set aside until frothy.

2 In a bowl, stir together the flours
and salt. Make a well in the center
and add the yeast liquid and oil. Mix
the flour into the liquid to make a
firm dough.

3 Turn the dough out onto a
lightly floured surface and knead for
about 10 minutes, until the dough
feels smooth and elastic and no
longer sticky.

4 Place the dough in a clean bowl,
cover with plastic wrap or a damp
kitchen towel, and leave in a warm
place until doubled in size —
about 45 minutes.

5 Turn the dough out onto a lightly
floured surface and knead again for
2-3 minutes.

6 Roll the dough out to a circle roughly
10 inches in diameter. Place on a baking
sheet, making the edges of the dough
slightly thicker than the center. The
pizza dough is now ready to complete
and bake with a delicious topping.

VARIATION
● Stir 3-4 tbsp chopped fresh herbs or
2-3 tsp dried mixed herbs into the
flour before making the dough.

PIZZA

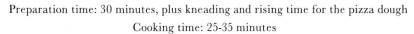

Preparation time: 30 minutes, plus kneading and rising time for the pizza dough

Cooking time: 25-35 minutes

Serves 6

1 quantity pizza dough (see page 37)
1 red bell pepper
1 green bell pepper
1 yellow bell pepper
1 tsp olive oil
1 small onion, sliced
1¹/₂ cups mushrooms, sliced
1 recipe tomato sauce (see page 37)
2 tbsp chopped fresh mixed herbs or 2 tsp dried herbs
¹/₄ cup shredded mozzarella cheese
2 tbsp finely grated Parmesan cheese
fresh herb sprigs, to garnish

1 Prepare and shape the pizza dough as explained in the recipe on page 37.

2 Place the bell peppers under a hot broiler and cook for 10-15 minutes, until the skin is charred and black. Plunge the bell peppers into cold water — the skins will rub off between your fingers. Pat dry. Core, seed, and slice the bell peppers.

3 Meanwhile, heat the oil in a saucepan, add the onion and mushrooms, and cook gently for 5-10 minutes, stirring occasionally, until the vegetables are beginning to soften.

4 Spread the tomato sauce evenly over the pizza base, then sprinkle the mixed herbs over the top.

NUTRITIONAL ANALYSIS

(figures are per serving)

Calories = 241
Fat = 6.9g
of which saturates = 2.6g
    monounsaturates = 2.7g
    polyunsaturates = 0.9g
Protein = 11.7g
Carbohydrate = 35.4g
Dietary fiber = 5.0g
Sodium = 0.3g

Percentage of total calories from fat = 26%
of which saturates = 9%
Good source of vitamin C

5 Arrange the bell peppers, onions, and mushrooms over the tomato sauce.

6 Sprinkle the mozzarella cheese over the pizza, then sprinkle the Parmesan cheese over the top.

7 Bake in a preheated oven at 425°, for 25-35 minutes, until the dough is risen and the pizza is golden brown.

8 Garnish with fresh herb sprigs and serve hot or cold in slices with a mixed side salad.

VARIATIONS

● Use other vegetables such as zucchini in place of the mushrooms.
● Use reduced-fat hard cheese such as Cheddar or Monterey jack cheese in place of the mozzarella.
● Use 4 shallots, 1 red onion, or 1 leek in place of the onion.

SMOKED HAM, TOMATO, &
BASIL PIZZA

Preparation time: 25 minutes, plus kneading and rising time for the pizza dough

Cooking time: 25-35 minutes

Serves 6

1 quantity pizza dough (see page 37)
1 quantity tomato sauce (see page 37)
2-3 tbsp chopped fresh basil
1 cup diced cooked, lean, smoked ham
4 tomatoes, sliced
*¹/₄ cup finely grated
reduced-fat mature
Cheddar cheese*
*¹/₄ cup finely shredded
mozzarella cheese*
*fresh basil leaves,
to garnish*

1 Prepare and shape the pizza dough as instructed on page 37.

2 Spread the tomato sauce evenly over the pizza base, then sprinkle the basil over the top.

3 Scatter the ham over the sauce and top with the tomato slices.

4 Mix the yellow cheese and mozzarella together and sprinkle over the pizza.

5 Bake the pizza in a preheated oven at 425° for 25-35 minutes, until the dough is risen and the pizza is golden-brown in color.

6 Garnish with fresh basil leaves and serve hot or cold in slices with seasonal fresh vegetables.

VARIATIONS

● Use any kind of lean smoked meat in place of the smoked ham.
● Use mixed herbs in place of the basil.
● Use other reduced-fat yellow cheese in place of the Cheddar.

NUTRITIONAL ANALYSIS

(figures are per serving)

Calories = 263
Fat = 6.8g
of which saturates = 2.7g
     monounsaturates = 2.4g
     polyunsaturates = 0.8g
Protein = 18.7g
Carbohydrate = 33.4g
Dietary fiber = 3.6g
Sodium = 0.3g

Percentage of total calories from fat = 23%
of which saturates = 9%

ORIENTAL VEGETABLE STIR-FRY

This colorful mixture of fresh, crispy vegetables tossed in a light sweet-and-sour sauce makes a nutritious yet quick and easy stir-fry dinner or snack.

Preparation time: 20 minutes

Cooking time: 8-10 minutes

Serves 4

1 tbsp white wine or rice wine
1 tsp grated ginger root
2 tsp cornstarch
4 tbsp unsweetened apple juice
2 tbsp light soft brown sugar
2 tbsp light soy sauce
1 tbsp tomato ketchup
1 tbsp white wine or rice vinegar
2 tsp sunflower oil
2 cloves garlic, crushed
2 leeks (trimmed weight), thinly sliced
1 red bell pepper, seeded and sliced
1 green bell pepper, seeded and sliced
3 carrots, cut into matchstick strips
1 cup mushrooms, sliced
$^{1}/_{2}$ cup snow-peas, trimmed
$^{1}/_{2}$ cup bean sprouts
14-ounce can corn, drained

1 Combine the wine and ginger root and leave to steep for at least 30 minutes. In a small bowl, blend the cornstarch with the apple juice until smooth. Add the wine and ginger mixture, sugar, soy sauce, tomato ketchup, and vinegar and mix well. Set aside.

2 Heat the oil in a large nonstick skillet or wok. Add the garlic and stir-fry over a high heat for 30 seconds.

3 Add the leeks, peppers, and carrots and stir-fry for 2-3 minutes. Add the remaining vegetables and stir-fry for 2-3 minutes.

4 Reduce the heat a little and add the sauce to the vegetables. Stir-fry until the

sauce comes to the boil and thickens, then cook for a further 1-2 minutes, stirring frequently.

5 Serve immediately on its own or with baked potatoes or a cooked mixture of brown and wild or pecan rice.

VARIATIONS
● Use your own choice of fresh vegetables.
● For the sauce, use unsweetened pineapple juice and sherry in place of the apple juice and wine.
● Sprinkle the stir-fry with toasted sesame seeds or shelled sunflower seeds just before serving.

CHEESE-TOPPED VEGETABLES
PROVENÇAL

*This combination of braised fresh vegetables with a crispy, cheese topping is
ideal served with boiled pasta, baked potatoes, or thick slices of fresh bread.
Try serving it as an accompaniment to broiled lean meat or fish as an entrée.*

Preparation time: 20 minutes

Cooking time: 20-25 minutes

Serves 6

4 cups tomatoes, skinned and chopped
4 zucchini, sliced
3 leeks trimmed and sliced
1¹/₄ cups button mushrooms
1 onion, sliced
1 red bell pepper, seeded and sliced
1 yellow bell pepper, seeded and sliced
1 clove garlic, crushed
*14-ounce can chick-peas (garbanzo beans), rinsed
and drained*
²/₃ cup tomato juice
1 tbsp tomato paste
1 tbsp tomato ketchup
1 tbsp chopped fresh rosemary
salt and freshly ground black pepper
*¹/₂ cup finely grated reduced-fat
mature yellow cheese*
4 tbsp fresh whole-wheat bread crumbs
fresh herb sprigs, to garnish

1 Place all the ingredients, except the
cheese, whole-wheat bread crumbs, and
herb sprigs, in a saucepan and mix well.

2 Cover, bring to the boil, and cook
gently for 15-20 minutes, until the
vegetables are just tender, stirring
occasionally.

3 Transfer the vegetable mixture to a
shallow, ovenproof serving dish.

4 Mix together the cheese and bread
crumbs and sprinkle over the vegetables.
Cook under a preheated medium broiler
until the cheese has melted and the
topping is crispy.

5 Garnish with fresh herb sprigs, such as
rosemary or thyme.

VARIATIONS
● Use your own choice of fresh
vegetables.
● Use other canned beans such as kidney
or lima beans in place of the chick-peas
(garbanzo beans).
● Use fresh mixed herbs or fresh thyme
in place of the rosemary.

NUTRITIONAL ANALYSIS

(figures are per serving)

Calories = 192
Fat = 5.5g
of which   saturates = 2.2g
    monounsaturates = 1.3g
    polyunsaturates = 1.3g

Protein = 14.0g
Carbohydrate = 23.2g
Dietary fiber = 6.2g
Sodium = 0.3g

Percentage of total calories from fat = 26%, of which saturates = 10%
Good source of vitamins A & C

CHAPTER FOUR

ENTRÉES

*W*hether you eat your main meal at lunchtime, teatime, or in the evening,
*it will be, by definition, your most substantial meal of the day, and it is
therefore important to make it as appetizing and nutritious as possible.
Here are mouthwatering meals that are quick and easy both
to prepare and cook, and are ideal for everyday cooking, such as stir-fries
and casseroles. Additionally, there are grander dishes for special occasions and for
serving to guests, such as stuffed fish or a savory choux ring.
Also included are meals for out-of-doors cooking, such as kabobs, as well as
a selection of vegetarian meals that make an interesting and flavorful
change from meat- or fish-based meals.*

BAKED COD
WITH WATERCRESS SAUCE

*Fresh cod steaks are baked until just cooked and tender, and served with a
light watercress — an ideal dish for the family or for guests.*

Preparation time: 25 minutes

Cooking time: 20-30 minutes

Serves 4

*4 cod steaks, each weighing about 8 ounces
juice of 1 lemon
2 tbsp chopped fresh mixed herbs
salt and freshly ground black pepper
1 small onion, minced
1 clove garlic, crushed
1/3 cup chopped watercress
2/3 cup vegetable broth
2 tbsp low-fat spread
2 tbsp all-purpose flour
1 1/2 cups skim milk
2 tbsp finely grated reduced-fat mature Cheddar
or Monterey jack cheese*

1 Lightly grease 4 pieces of aluminum
foil large enough to hold each cod steak.
Place a cod steak on each piece of foil,
sprinkle with lemon juice, herbs, and
seasoning, and fold up loosely in the foil.

2 Place on a cookie sheet and bake
in a preheated oven at 350° for
20-30 minutes.

3 Meanwhile, make the watercress
sauce. Place the onion, garlic,
watercress, and broth in a saucepan and
stir to mix.

4 Cover and cook gently for 5 minutes.

5 Remove from the heat and allow to
cool slightly, then place in a blender or
food processor and blend until smooth.

6 Place the low-fat spread, flour, and
milk in a saucepan and heat gently,
whisking continuously, until the sauce
comes to the boil and thickens. Simmer
gently for 3 minutes, stirring.

7 Add the watercress purée and mix
well. Reheat gently, stirring.

8 Remove the pan from the heat, add
the cheese and seasoning, and stir until
well-blended.

9 Serve the cod steaks with the sauce
poured over.

SPICY SHRIMP & MUSHROOM
PHYLLO CLUSTERS

Serve these deliciously light and crispy phyllo clusters with baked potatoes and seasonal fresh vegetables such as cauliflower and broccoli flowerets.

Preparation time: 25 minutes
Cooking time: 25-30 minutes
Serves 4 (2 clusters per serving)

FOR THE FILLING
1 bunch green onions (scallions), chopped
3/4 cup minced mushrooms
3/4 cup small peeled bay shrimp
4 sun-dried tomatoes, soaked, drained, and finely chopped
1/2-inch piece fresh root ginger, peeled and minced or grated
1 clove garlic, crushed
1/2 tsp hot chili powder or 1 small red chili, seeded and finely chopped
1 tsp ground coriander (cilantro)
2 tbsp chopped fresh coriander (cilantro)
1 tbsp fresh Parmesan cheese, finely grated
salt and freshly ground black pepper

8 sheets phyllo dough
2 tbsp sunflower oil
fresh coriander (cilantro), to garnish

1 Place all the ingredients for the filling in a bowl and mix together thoroughly. Set aside.

2 To make each phyllo cluster, cut each sheet of phyllo dough in half crosswise to make two squares or rectangles (a total of 16 squares or rectangles), depending on the shape of the sheet.

3 Lightly brush 2 squares of dough with oil and place one on top of the other diagonally. Place some shrimp filling in the center of the dough.

4 Gather up the dough over the filling and secure with string. Place the cluster on a cookie sheet lined with nonstick baking paper and brush lightly with oil.

5 Repeat with the remaining dough squares and filling to make 8 clusters.

6 Bake in a preheated oven at 400° for 25-30 minutes, until golden brown and crisp.

7 Carefully remove the string from each cluster before serving. Garnish with fresh coriander (cilantro) leaves.

VARIATIONS
● Use other cooked, shelled seafood such as mussels or clams in place of the shrimp.
● Use other spices such as curry powder or cumin in place of the chili powder or coriander (cilantro).
● Use other fresh herbs such as mixed herbs or parsley in place of the coriander (cilantro).

SALMON STEAKS
WITH CUCUMBER RELISH

*A refreshing cucumber relish makes an interesting
addition to this dish of succulent salmon steaks.*

Preparation time: 15 minutes, plus standing time for the relish

Cooking time: 8 minutes

Serves 6

1 large or 2 small cucumbers
1 large red onion
3 tbsp chopped fresh coriander (cilantro)
juice of 2 limes
salt and freshly ground black pepper
¹/₂ tsp sugar
6 salmon steaks, each weighing about 4 ounces
lime rind strips, to garnish

1 To make the relish, cut the cucumber in half lengthwise, and remove and discard the seeds. Finely dice the cucumber and place in a bowl.

2 Peel the onion and mince it. Add it to the cucumber with the coriander (cilantro), lime juice, seasoning, and sugar. Mix thoroughly, cover, and set aside for a couple of hours, to allow the flavors to develop.

3 To cook the salmon, place it on a broiler pan and broil under medium heat for about 8 minutes, turning once, until the salmon is cooked and is just beginning to flake.

4 Garnish with strips of lime rind and serve with the cucumber relish, accompanied by boiled new potatoes and a green side salad.

VARIATIONS
● The salmon may be cooked over a barbecue or charbroiled.
● Use other chopped fresh herbs such as mixed herbs in place of the coriander (cilantro).
● Use lemon juice in place of the lime juice.

NUTRITIONAL ANALYSIS

*(including the cucumber relish and a portion of green salad and new
potatoes per serving – figures are per serving)*

Calories = 351
Fat = 12.9g
of which saturates = 2.5g
          monounsaturates = 5.3g
          polyunsaturates = 4.1g

Protein = 26.6g
Carbohydrate = 33.8g
Dietary fiber = 3.2g
Sodium = 0.07g

Percentage of total calories from fat = 33%, of which saturates = 6%
Good source of B vitamins

RAINBOW TROUT
WITH PARSLEY & LIME STUFFING

This recipe captures all the delicious juices and flavor of trout by baking them in individual packages.

Preparation time: 20 minutes

Cooking time: 20-30 minutes

Serves 4

4 rainbow trout, each weighing about 10 ounces, gutted and cleaned but with heads and tails left on

FOR THE STUFFING
1 tsp olive oil
1 onion, minced
³/₄ cup mushrooms, finely chopped
2 limes
4 tbsp medium raw oatmeal
4 tbsp fresh whole-wheat bread crumbs
1 tart apple, peeled, cored, and coarsely grated
1 egg white
3 tbsp chopped fresh parsley
salt and freshly ground black pepper
fresh herb sprigs, to garnish

1 Rinse the fish under cold running water and pat dry with paper towels. Set aside.

2 To make the stuffing, heat the oil in a saucepan, add the onion and mushrooms, and cook for 5 minutes, stirring occasionally. Grate the rind from the limes.

3 Remove the pan from the heat, add the grated lime rind and the remaining stuffing ingredients, and mix well.

4 Spoon some of the stuffing into the cavity of each trout, dividing it up equally.

5 Lightly grease 4 pieces of aluminum foil large enough to hold each fish in a package. Place a fish on each piece of foil, sprinkle with lime juice, and seal the packages.

6 Place the packages in a roasting pan and bake at 350° for 20-30 minutes, until the fish is cooked and is just beginning to flake.

7 Transfer the packages to serving dishes and open the tops of the packages. Garnish the trout with fresh herb sprigs such as parsley or dill and serve with seasonal fresh vegetables such as boiled new potatoes, baby carrots, and zucchini.

VARIATIONS
● Stuff other whole fish, such as mackerel or catfish, in place of the trout.
● Use lemon rind and juice in place of the lime rind and juice.
● Use other fresh herbs such as mixed herbs or coriander (cilantro) in place of the parsley.

NUTRITIONAL ANALYSIS

(figures are per serving)

Calories = 380
Fat = 13.1g
of which saturates = 2.6g
    monounsaturates = 4.7g
    polyunsaturates = 4.3g
Protein = 44g
Carbohydrate = 23.2g
Dietary fiber = 3.7g
Sodium = 0.2g

Percentage of total calories from fat = 31%
of which saturates = 6%
Good source of protein & B vitamins

SPICY ROAST
CHICKEN

An appetizing way of serving roast chicken that contains little fat but plenty of flavor and color.

Preparation time: 10 minutes

Cooking time: 30-45 minutes

Serves 4

1 tbsp olive oil
juice of ¹/₂ lemon or lime
1 clove garlic, crushed
1 tsp ground coriander (cilantro)
1 tsp ground cumin
1 tsp hot chili powder
salt and freshly ground black pepper
4 skinless, boneless chicken breasts
chopped fresh coriander (cilantro) sprigs,
to garnish

1 Place the oil, lemon or lime juice, garlic, spices, and seasoning in a bowl and whisk together until thoroughly mixed.

2 Place each chicken breast on a piece of parchment paper large enough to hold each chicken breast in a package.

3 Slash each piece of chicken diagonally across the top and brush with some of the spicy mixture.

4 Fold the paper loosely over each chicken breast and twist the edges together to seal tightly, making a total of 4 packages. Place the packages on a baking sheet.

5 Bake in a preheated oven at 400° for 30-45 minutes, until cooked and tender.

6 Undo the packages and place the chicken breasts on warmed serving dishes. Pour any juices over the chicken and garnish with chopped coriander (cilantro).

7 Serve immediately with a crunchy, mixed vegetable stir-fry.

VARIATION
● Use flavored oil such as chili or herb oil in place of the olive oil.

NUTRITIONAL ANALYSIS
(figures are per serving)

Calories = 184

Fat = 4.6g

of which saturates = 0.8g

    monounsaturates = 2.8g

    polyunsaturates = 0.5g

Protein = 36.2g

Carbohydrate = 0.04g

Dietary fiber = 0g

Sodium = 0.1g

Percentage of total calories from fat = 23%

of which saturates = 4%

QUICK & EASY
SAUCES

CHEESE & CHIVE
Follow the Chicken & Mustard Sauce recipe but add 4 tbsp finely grated reduced-fat mature Cheddar cheese and 2-3 tbsp chopped fresh chives to the cooked sauce in place of the mustard.

PARSLEY OR TARRAGON
Follow the Chicken & Mustard Sauce recipe but add 2-3 tbsp chopped fresh parsley or fresh tarragon to the cooked sauce in place of the mustard.

SAGE & ONION
Follow the Chicken & Mustard Sauce recipe but add 1-2 tbsp chopped fresh sage and 1 blanced, minced onion to the cooked sauce in place of the mustard.

CAPER
Follow the Chicken & Mustard Sauce recipe but add 1-2 tbsp chopped capers and 1-2 tsp of the vinegar from the capers to the cooked sauce in place of the mustard.

MUSHROOM
Follow the Chicken & Mustard Sauce recipe but add $^3/_4$-1 cup mushrooms, chopped or sliced and blanched, to the cooked sauce in place of the mustard.

NUTRITIONAL ANALYSIS
(figures are per serving)

Calories = 233
Fat = 6.5g
of which saturates = 1.3g
   monounsaturates = 3g
   polyunsaturates = 1g

Protein = 38.4g
Carbohydrate = 5.5g
Dietary fiber = 0.3g
Sodium = 0.6g

Percentage of total calories from fat = 25%
of which saturates = 5%

CHICKEN & MUSTARD SAUCE

Juicy, tender, oven-baked chicken breasts are spiced up in this recipe with a tangy mustard sauce.

Preparation time: 15 minutes
Cooking time: 30-45 minutes
Serves 4

1 tbsp olive oil
1 tbsp light soy sauce
juice of 1 lemon
2 tbsp chopped fresh mixed herbs
salt and freshly ground black pepper
4 skinless, boneless chicken breasts
1 tbsp low-fat spread
1 tbsp all-purpose flour
$^2/_3$ cup skim milk
$^2/_3$ cup chicken broth, cooled
1 tbsp whole-grain mustard
fresh herb sprigs, to garnish

1 Whisk together the oil, soy sauce, lemon juice, herbs, and seasoning. Place each chicken breast on a piece of parchment paper large enough to hold it in a package. Spoon some of the herb mixture over each piece of chicken.

2 Fold over the paper and twist the edges together to seal. Place on a cookie sheet and bake in a preheated oven at 400° for 30-45 minutes, until cooked and tender.

3 Meanwhile, make the mustard sauce. Place the low-fat spread, flour, milk, and broth in a saucepan and heat gently, whisking continuously, until the sauce comes to the boil and thickens. Simmer gently for 3 minutes, stirring.

4 Add the mustard and seasoning and mix well.

5 Serve the cooked chicken breasts with the mustard sauce poured over. Garnish with fresh herb sprigs.

VARIATIONS
● Use turkey breasts in place of the chicken breasts.
● Use lime in place of the lemon juice.

QUICK & EASY STIR-FRIES

Stir-frying is a very quick and easy method of cooking and combining many foods and ingredients, to create colorful and nutritious meals in just a few minutes. This method of cooking seals in the food's natural juices, and ensures that it stays crisp and keeps its flavor as well as its nutrients.

Extend your repertoire by stir-frying other complementary combinations of ingredients, such as peppered beef with snow-peas, crunchy cabbage and wild mushrooms, beef with garlic and ginger, stir-fried baby vegetables, oriental pork and vegetables, sweet-and-sour shrimp, or hot and spicy chicken.

LAMB & VEGETABLE STIR-FRY

Tender lamb and crispy vegetables are subtly flavored with an oriental spice mix in this tasty stir-fry.

Preparation time: 15 minutes
Cooking time: 9-12 minutes
Serves 4

2 tsp cornstarch
2 tbsp light soy sauce
2 tbsp dry sherry
1 tbsp tomato paste
²/₃ cup vegetable or beef broth, cooled
1 tsp five-spice powder
salt and freshly ground black pepper
8 ounces lean lamb, cut into thin strips
1 bunch green onions (scallions), chopped
1 clove garlic, crushed
1 red bell pepper, seeded and sliced
1 yellow bell pepper, seeded and sliced
1 cup small broccoli flowerets
4 carrots, cut into matchstick strips
1¹/₄ cups sliced mushrooms
³/₄ cup bean sprouts
³/₄ cup snow-peas, trimmed

1 In a small bowl, blend the cornstarch with the soy sauce. Add the sherry, tomato paste, broth, five-spice powder, and seasoning and mix well. Set aside.

2 Heat a large nonstick skillet or wok. Add the lamb, green onions (scallions), and garlic, and stir-fry over a medium heat for 2-3 minutes.

3 Add the bell peppers, broccoli, and carrots and stir-fry for 3-4 minutes.

4 Add the remaining vegetables and stir-fry for a further 2-3 minutes. Lower the heat, add the cornstarch mixture, and stir-fry until the sauce is thickened and glossy. Simmer for 2 minutes, stirring frequently.

5 Serve immediately on a bed of boiled brown and pecan rice or bulghur wheat with a mixed green side salad.

VARIATIONS

● Use other lean meat such as beef, pork, chicken, or turkey in place of the lamb.
● Use your own choice of mixed vegetables.
● Use applejack, brandy, or unsweetened apple juice in place of the sherry.
● Use chili or curry powder in place of the five-spice powder.

NUTRITIONAL ANALYSIS

(figures are per serving)

Calories = 200
Fat = 6.2g
of which saturates = 2.4g
monounsaturates = 1.9g
polyunsaturates = 1g
Protein = 18.4g
Carbohydrate = 16.6g
Dietary fiber = 6.2g
Sodium = 0.7g

Percentage of total calories from fat = 28%
of which saturates = 10%

STIR-FRIED TURKEY WITH
SPRING VEGETABLES

Young, spring vegetables bring an array of contrasting textures to this stimulating stir-fry.

Preparation time: 15 minutes
Cooking time: 8-12 minutes
Serves 4

2 tbsp dry sherry
2 tbsp light soy sauce
4 tbsp fresh tomato juice
1 tbsp chili sauce
1 tsp chili powder (optional)
salt and freshly ground black pepper
2 tsp sunflower oil
1 clove garlic, crushed
12 ounces skinless, boneless turkey breast, cut into thin strips
1 bunch green onions (scallions), chopped
2 carrots, cut into matchstick strips
1 cup rutabaga, cut into matchstick strips
1 red bell pepper, seeded and diced
³/₄ cup green beans, trimmed and halved
4 zucchini, peeled and thinly sliced
³/₄ cup bean sprouts
³/₄ cup broccoli flowerets or collard greens, chopped
chopped fresh mixed herbs, to garnish

1 In a bowl, mix together the sherry, soy sauce, tomato juice, chili sauce, chili powder (if using), and seasoning. Set aside.

2 Heat the oil in a large nonstick skillet or wok. Add the garlic and stir-fry over a high heat for 10 seconds. Add the turkey and stir-fry for 2-3 minutes.

3 Add the green onions (scallions), carrots, rutabaga, bell pepper, and green beans, and stir-fry for 3-4 minutes.

4 Add the remaining vegetables and stir-fry for 2-3 minutes.

5 Add the sherry mixture and stir-fry for 1-2 minutes, until the sauce is hot and bubbling.

6 Garnish with chopped fresh herbs and serve immediately with cooked egg noodles or fresh, crusty bread.

VARIATIONS

● Use other lean meats such as chicken, pork, or beef or cooked, peeled shrimp in place of the turkey.
● Use mushrooms and cauliflower in place of the green beans and zucchini.
● Use curry sauce and curry powder in place of the chili sauce and chili powder, for a change.

NUTRITIONAL ANALYSIS

(figures are per serving)

Calories = 205
Fat = 3.5g
of which saturates = 0.8g
monounsaturates = 1.4g
polyunsaturates = 1g
Protein = 26.5g
Carbohydrate = 15.5g
Dietary fiber = 5.3g
Sodium = 0.7g

Percentage of total calories from fat = 15%
of which saturates = 3%
Good source of vitamins A, C, & B vitamins

COQ AU VIN

Preparation time: 25 minutes

Cooking time: 1½-2 hours

Serves 4

2 skinless chicken leg joints
2 skinless chicken breast joints
2 slices smoked lean bacon, trimmed and diced
1½ cups shallots or button onions, peeled
6 carrots, sliced
1¼ cups dry red wine
1¼ cups chicken broth
1 tbsp tomato paste
2 small cloves garlic, crushed
salt and freshly ground black pepper
1 bouquet garni (thyme, bay leaf,
and parsley tied together)
1¼ cups button mushrooms
1½ tbsp cornstarch

1 Place the chicken joints in a large, flameproof, ovenproof casserole dish

with the bacon, shallots or button onions, and carrots.

2 Mix together the wine, broth, tomato paste, garlic, and seasoning and pour over the chicken and vegetables. Add the bouquet garni and mix.

3 Cook in a preheated oven at 350° for 1 hour. Add the mushrooms and stir gently to mix.

4 Cook for a further 30-60 minutes.

5 Remove the chicken. Place on a serving platter, cover, and keep hot.

6 Discard the bouquet garni. Blend the cornstarch with 3 tbsp water and stir into the juices and vegetables in the casserole. Bring to the boil, stirring, until thickened, then simmer for 3 minutes, stirring.

7 Spoon the vegetables and sauce over the chicken and serve.

VARIATIONS
● Use white wine in place of the red.
● Use 1 large sliced onion in place of the shallots.

NUTRITIONAL ANALYSIS

(figures are per serving)

Calories = 279
Fat = 3.4g
of which saturates = 0.9g
 monounsaturates = 1g
 polyunsaturates = 0.8g
Protein = 36.1g
Carbohydrate = 14.3g
Dietary fiber = 4.1g
Sodium = 0.6g

Percentage of total calories from fat = 11%
of which saturates = 3%
Good source of vitamin A

BEEF & VEGETABLE
KABOBS

Cubes of lean beef and crispy fresh vegetables are broiled or barbecued to perfection for a memorable summer meal alfresco.

Preparation time: 20 minutes

Cooking time: 8-12 minutes

Serves 4 (2 kabobs per serving)

12 ounces lean topside, tenderloin, or sirloin steak, trimmed of fat
1 small green bell pepper
1 small red bell pepper
1 small yellow bell pepper
1 zucchini
16 button onions, peeled
16 button mushrooms
16 cherry tomatoes
4 bay leaves (optional)
1 tbsp olive oil
juice of 1 orange
1 tsp dried thyme
salt and freshly ground black pepper

1 Cut the beef into 24 small cubes and set aside. Cut the bell peppers in half, and remove and discard the seeds. Cut each half into 4 squares (making a total of 8 squares per bell pepper). Slice the zucchini into 16 slices.

2 Thread the beef, bell peppers, zucchini, onions, mushrooms, and tomatoes onto

8 skewers, dividing the ingredients equally between the kabobs. Thread a bay leaf onto the end of 4 of the skewers, if using.

3 Beat together the oil, orange juice, thyme, and seasoning and brush the mixture over the kabobs.

4 Cook the kabobs over a barbecue or under a preheated broiler on medium heat for about 8-12 minutes, turning frequently, until the beef is cooked to your liking. Brush the kabobs with any remaining oil mixture while they are cooking, to prevent them from drying out.

5 Serve with slices of fresh crusty bread and a green side salad.

VARIATIONS
● Use other lean meats such as chicken, turkey, or pork in place of the beef.
● Use other vegetables or fruit such as baby corn or pineapple cubes.
● Use curry powder, ground cumin, or chili powder in place of the thyme.
● Twist sprigs of thyme around the kabobs.

NUTRITIONAL ANALYSIS

(figures are per serving)

Calories = 199

Fat = 7.1g

of which   saturates = 2.1g

    monounsaturates = 3.6g

    polyunsaturates = 0.9g

Protein = 22.3g

Carbohydrate = 12.3g

Dietary fiber = 3.3g

Sodium = 0.06g

Percentage of total calories from fat = 32%, of which saturates = 9%

Good source of B vitamins & vitamin C

MEDITERRANEAN VEGETABLE
LASAGNA

A nutritious vegetarian version of the traditional meat-based dish, this lasagna is packed with flavor and appetizing color.

Preparation time: 30 minutes

Cooking time: 45-60 minutes

Serves 6

NUTRITIONAL ANALYSIS
(figures are per serving)

Calories = 263
Fat = 7.3g
of which saturates = 2.9g
    monounsaturates = 1g
    polyunsaturates = 1.7g
Protein = 15.6g
Carbohydrate = 35.9g
Dietary fiber = 4.7g
Sodium = 0.3g

Percentage of total calories from fat = 25%
of which saturates = 9%
Good source of calcium & vitamin A

1 onion, sliced
1 red onion, sliced
1 clove garlic, crushed
1 red bell pepper, seeded and sliced
1 yellow bell pepper, seeded and sliced
1 1/2 cups sliced zucchini
1 cup sliced brown cap mushrooms
1 cup sliced white cap mushrooms
3 cups skinned and chopped plum tomatoes
4 tbsp fresh tomato juice
1 tbsp tomato paste
2 tbsp chopped fresh mixed herbs such as oregano, rosemary, and thyme
salt and freshly ground pepper
3 tbsp low-fat spread
3 tbsp all-purpose flour
1/2 tsp smooth mustard
1 1/4 cups skim milk
1 1/4 cups vegetable broth
1/2 cup finely grated reduced-fat mature Cheddar cheese
6 ounces green lasagna (no pre-cook variety)
mixed salad leaves, to garnish

1 Place the onions, garlic, bell peppers, zucchini, mushrooms, tomatoes, fresh tomato juice, and tomato paste in a large saucepan. Cover and cook for 10 minutes, stirring occasionally. Add the herbs and seasoning, and mix well.

2 Meanwhile, make the cheese sauce. Place the low-fat spread, flour, mustard, milk, and broth in a saucepan. Heat gently, whisking continuously, until the sauce comes to the boil and thickens. Simmer gently for 3 minutes, stirring.

3 Remove the pan from the heat, add half the cheese and seasoning, and mix well.

4 Assemble the lasagna. Spoon half the vegetable mixture in a shallow pie pan or ovenproof dish. Cover this with half the pasta and top with one third of the cheese sauce.

5 Repeat these layers, topping with the remaining cheese sauce to cover the pasta completely. Sprinkle the remaining cheese over the top.

6 Bake the lasagna in a preheated oven at 350° for 45-60 minutes, until cooked and golden brown on top.

7 Garnish with mixed salad leaves and serve with low-calorie coleslaw and fresh crusty bread.

VARIATIONS
● Use your own choice of mixed vegetables for this lasagna.
● Use white or whole-wheat lasagna in place of the green lasagna.
● Use other reduced-fat hard cheese such as Monterey jack in place of the Cheddar.
● Use one 14-ounce can peeled, chopped tomatoes in place of the fresh tomatoes.
● Use whole-grain mustard in place of the smooth mustard.

EGGPLANT, TOMATO, & ZUCCHINI
PASTA BAKE

Preparation time: 30 minutes, plus standing time for the eggplant

Cooking time: 30 minutes

Serves 6

1¹/₂ cups sliced eggplant
salt and freshly ground black pepper
1 onion, sliced
2 leeks, washed and thinly sliced
1 clove garlic, crushed
1 cup sliced zucchini
1 cup sliced yellow zucchini or summer squash
14-ounce can peeled, chopped tomatoes
1 tbsp tomato paste
1 tbsp tomato ketchup
8 ounces short macaroni
2 tbsp low-fat spread
2 tbsp all-purpose flour
2¹/₂ cups skim milk
14-ounce can chick-peas (garbanzo beans), rinsed and drained
3 tbsp chopped fresh mixed herbs
6 tbsp finely grated reduced-fat Monterey jack cheese
2 tbsp fresh whole-wheat bread crumbs

1 Sprinkle the eggplant slices with salt and leave to stand for about 30 minutes, to extract the bitter juices. Rinse thoroughly under cold running water and pat dry with paper towels.

2 Place the eggplant, onion, leeks, garlic, zucchini, tomatoes, tomato paste, and tomato ketchup in a large saucepan and stir to mix.

3 Cover and cook gently for 20 minutes, stirring occasionally.

4 Meanwhile, cook the macaroni in a large saucepan of lightly salted, boiling water for 8 minutes, until just tender. Drain thoroughly and keep warm.

5 In the meantime, make the white sauce. Place the low-fat spread, flour, and milk in a saucepan. Heat gently, whisking continuously, until the sauce comes to the boil and thickens. Simmer gently for 3 minutes, stirring.

6 Add the chick-peas (garbanzo beans), herbs, and seasoning and stir to mix.

7 Stir the vegetable mixture, macaroni, and white sauce together and place in a large ovenproof casserole dish. Mix the cheese and bread crumbs together and sprinkle evenly over the top.

8 Bake in a preheated oven at 375° for about 30 minutes, until lightly browned and bubbling. Serve with a crisp green side salad.

VARIATIONS
● Use your own choice of mixed vegetables for this pasta bake.
● Use other shapes of pasta, such as twists or shell, in place of the macaroni.

NUTRITIONAL ANALYSIS
(figures are per serving)

Calories = 313
Fat = 6.8g
of which saturates = 2.3g
    monounsaturates = 1.1g
    polyunsaturates = 1.8g
Protein = 18.9g
Carbohydrate = 46.8g
Dietary fiber = 6.8g
Sodium = 0.4g

Percentage of total calories from fat = 20%
of which saturates = 7%

RATATOUILLE
RING

*In this recipe, a crispy, cheese-flavored choux pastry
ring surrounds a classic mixture of lightly braised vegetables.*

Preparation time: 25 minutes

Cooking time: 30-40 minutes

Serves 6

NUTRITIONAL ANALYSIS

(figures are per serving)

Calories = 177

Fat = 7g

of which saturates = 2.1g

monounsaturates = 1.2g

polyunsaturates = 1.7g

Protein − 8.6g

Carbohydrate = 20.3g

Dietary fiber = 4g

Sodium = 0.07g

Percentage of total calories
from fat = 35%
of which saturates = 10%
Good source of vitamins A & C

FOR THE PASTRY RING
5 tbsp all-purpose flour
4 tbsp low-fat spread
2 eggs, beaten
*2 tbsp finely grated reduced-fat mature Cheddar
cheese*

FOR THE RATATOUILLE
2 onions, sliced
2 cloves garlic, crushed
1 red bell pepper, seeded and cut into large dice
1 green bell pepper, seeded and cut into large dice
1 yellow bell pepper, seeded and cut into large dice
4 small zucchini, cut into small chunks
1 cup button mushrooms
4 medium tomatoes, skinned and roughly chopped
2 tbsp dry red wine
1 tbsp tomato paste
2 tsp dried mixed herbs
salt and freshly ground black pepper

fresh parsley sprigs, to garnish

1 To make the pastry ring, sift the flour
onto a plate. Place the low-fat spread
and ²/₃ cup water in a saucepan. Heat
gently until the fat has melted, then
bring to the boil.

2 Remove the pan from the heat and tip
the flour all at once into the hot liquid.
Beat thoroughly with a wooden spoon,
until the mixture forms a ball in the
center of the pan. Leave to cool slightly.

3 Beat the eggs in gradually, using a
wooden spoon or electric hand-whisk,
adding only enough to give the right
consistency for piping the mixture
through a forcing bag, beating the
mixture thoroughly after each addition.
Beat in the cheese.

4 Spoon or pipe the mixture in a ring
around the edges of a lightly greased
9-inch ovenproof dish.

5 Bake in a preheated oven at 425° for
30-40 minutes, until well-risen and
golden brown.

6 Meanwhile, make the ratatouille
filling. Place all the ratatouille
ingredients in a saucepan and stir to mix.

7 Cover, bring to the boil, and cook
gently for 20-30 minutes, stirring
occasionally, until the vegetables are
tender but not overcooked. Remove the
lid for the last 10 minutes of the cooking
time and increase the heat, to reduce the
liquid slightly, if the mixture is too liquid.

8 Spoon the ratatouille sauce into the
center of the ring. Garnish with fresh
parsley sprigs and serve with a crisp
side salad.

*The ratatouille sauce is suitable for cooking in
a microwave oven, and is also suitable for
freezing.*

VARIATIONS
● Use one 14-ounce can peeled, chopped
tomatoes in place of the fresh tomatoes.
● Use dry white wine or vermouth in
place of the red wine.
● Use other reduced-fat hard
cheese such as Monterey jack in place
of the Cheddar.

FARMHOUSE VEGETABLE
STEW

*Serve this stew of tender mixed vegetables with
a mixed green side salad and some crusty French bread.*

Preparation time: 15 minutes

Cooking time: 1¼-1½ hours

Serves 4

*1 onion, chopped
3 carrots, thinly sliced
3 leeks, washed and thinly sliced
1 turnip, thinly sliced
1 small rutabaga, finely diced
4 sticks celery, chopped
1¼ cups button mushrooms
14-ounce can peeled, chopped tomatoes
1 pound potatoes, washed and thinly sliced
1 tbsp olive oil
2 tbsp low-fat spread
2 tbsp all-purpose flour
⅔ cup vegetable broth, cooled
⅔ cup dry white wine
3 tbsp minced parsley
1 tbsp minced rosemary
salt and freshly ground black pepper
fresh herb sprigs, to garnish*

1 Place the onion, carrots, leeks, turnip,
rutabaga, celery, mushrooms, and
tomatoes in a saucepan and stir to mix.

2 Cover and cook gently for 25 minutes,
stirring occasionally.

3 Parboil the potatoes in a saucepan of
boiling water for 4 minutes. Drain
thoroughly, then toss the potato slices in
the oil. Set aside.

4 Meanwhile, make the sauce. Place the
low-fat spread, flour, broth, and wine in a
saucepan and heat gently, whisking
continuously, until the sauce comes to
the boil and thickens.

5 Simmer gently for 3 minutes,
stirring. Add to the cooked vegetables
with the chopped herbs and seasoning
and mix well.

6 Place the vegetable mixture in an
ovenproof casserole dish. Arrange the
potato slices over the vegetable mixture,
covering it completely.

7 Cover with foil and bake in a
preheated oven at 400° for 45-60
minutes, until the potatoes are cooked,
tender, and lightly browned on top.
Remove the foil for the last 20 minutes
of the cooking time.

8 Garnish with fresh herb sprigs and
serve immediately.

VARIATIONS
● Use sweet potatoes in place of the
standard potatoes.
● Use jicama in place of the turnip.
● Use red wine in place of the white
wine, or use grape juice.

NUTRITIONAL ANALYSIS

(figures are per serving)

Calories = 299
Fat = 7.4g
of which saturates = 1.3g
monounsaturates = 2.3g
polyunsaturates = 1.8g
Protein = 8.7g
Carbohydrate = 46.3g
Dietary fiber = 9.9g
Sodium = 0.2g

Percentage of total calories from fat = 22%
of which saturates = 4%
Good source of vitamins A & C

MUSHROOM
RISOTTO

Fresh chopped mixed herbs add vibrant flavor to this appetizing risotto, which is ideal served with some fresh crusty bread and a green side salad.

Preparation time: 15 minutes

Cooking time: 45 minutes

Serves 4

1 red onion, chopped
3 leeks, washed and thinly sliced
2 cloves garlic, crushed
1 red bell pepper, seeded and diced
4 sticks celery, chopped
1 cup long-grain brown rice
1¼ cups sliced mushrooms,
1¼ cups brown-cap mushrooms, sliced
2½ cups vegetable broth
1¼ cups dry white wine
salt and freshly ground black pepper
7-ounce can corn kernels, drained
½ cup frozen peas
3-4 tbsp chopped fresh mixed herbs
4 tbsp fresh Parmesan cheese shavings (optional)
fresh herb sprigs, to garnish

● Use red kidney beans or chick-peas (garbanzo beans) in place of the corn.
● Use fava beans or lima beans in place of the peas.

1 Place the onion, leeks, garlic, bell pepper, celery, rice, mushrooms, broth, wine, and seasoning in a large saucepan and stir to mix.

2 Bring to the boil and simmer, uncovered, for 25-30 minutes, stirring occasionally, until almost all the liquid has been absorbed.

3 Stir in the corn and peas and cook gently for about 10 minutes, stirring occasionally.

4 Stir in the chopped herbs and stir again to mix. Sprinkle with Parmesan cheese shavings, if using, and garnish with fresh herb sprigs.

VARIATIONS
● Use a mixture of edible wild mushrooms such as shiitake and oyster mushrooms for a change.
● Use finely grated Cheddar cheese in place of the Parmesan cheese shavings.

NUTRITIONAL ANALYSIS

(figures are per serving)

Calories = 448
Fat = 7.4g
of which saturates = 2.9g
      monounsaturates = 1.6g
      polyunsaturates = 1.8g
Protein = 15.5g
Carbohydrate = 72.5g
Dietary fiber = 7.3g
Sodium = 0.5g

Percentage of total calories from
fat = 15%
of which saturates = 6%
Good source of vitamin C

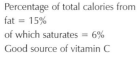

COUNTRY VEGETABLE & BARLEY
CASSEROLE

A warming and satisfying casserole for a comforting winter's day meal.

Preparation time: 15 minutes

Cooking time: 2 hours

Serves 4

2 tsp sunflower oil
1 onion, sliced
3 leeks, washed and sliced
1 clove garlic, crushed
1 pound new potatoes, washed
1 celery root, diced
3 carrots, sliced
2 turnips, sliced
1 cup button mushrooms
2 tbsp pearl barley
14-ounce can peeled, chopped tomatoes
2¹/₂ cups vegetable broth
2 tbsp tomato paste
1 bouquet garni
1 tsp ground coriander (cilantro)
salt and freshly ground black pepper
1-2 tbsp chopped fresh coriander (cilantro)
1-2 tbsp chopped fresh parsley

1 Heat the oil in a large ovenproof
casserole dish. Add the onion, leeks, and
garlic and cook for 5 minutes, stirring
occasionally.

2 Add all the remaining ingredients,
except the fresh herbs, and mix well.

3 Cover and bake in a preheated oven at
350° for about 2 hours, stirring
occasionally, until the vegetables and
barley are cooked and tender.

4 Stir in the chopped fresh herbs and
serve with crusty whole-wheat bread
and broiled lean meat or fish such as
chicken or cod.

VARIATIONS
● Use jicama and diced sweet potatoes
in place of the turnips and new potatoes.
● Use 4 skinned and chopped fresh
tomatoes in place of the canned
tomatoes.
● Use chopped fresh mixed herbs in
place of the coriander (cilantro)
and parsley.
● Use 2 tbsp long-grain brown
rice in place of
the barley.

NUTRITIONAL ANALYSIS

(figures are per serving)

Calories = 265
Fat = 4g
of which saturates = 0.6g
      monounsaturates = 1.4g
      polyunsaturates = 0.9g

Protein = 8.8g
Carbohydrate = 51.3g
Dietary fiber = 10.3g
Sodium = 0.4g

Percentage of total calories from fat = 14%, of which saturates = 2%
Good source of vitamin A & fiber

CHAPTER FIVE

SALADS & VEGETABLES

Salads and vegetables play an important part in meals, whether they are served as the main part or as an accompaniment to another dish. They also have a significant place in a healthy, well-balanced diet and contain important nutrients such as vitamins, minerals, and some fiber. Fresh vegetables and salad ingredients, as well as being nutritious, offer an infinite variety of flavors, textures, and colors, perfect for creating appetizing and delicious dishes for every occasion.

MIXED TOMATO &
PEPPER SALAD
WITH PARSLEY DRESSING

This colorful salad comprises fresh bell peppers and tomatoes tossed together in a light, herbed dressing. Serve with broiled lean meat or fish kabobs and warm pita bread.

Preparation time: 15 minutes

Serves 6

4 red plum tomatoes
4 yellow tomatoes
1 cup cherry tomatoes
1 red bell pepper, seeded and sliced into rings
1 yellow bell pepper, seeded and sliced into rings
1 large red onion, sliced into rings
4 sun-dried tomatoes, soaked, drained, and finely chopped

FOR THE DRESSING
6 tbsp low-fat plain yogurt
4 tbsp reduced-calorie mayonnaise
2 tsp whole-grain mustard
3-4 tbsp chopped fresh parsley
salt and freshly ground black pepper
fresh parsley sprigs, to garnish

1 Slice the plum tomatoes and the yellow tomatoes thinly, and halve the cherry tomatoes.

2 Place the tomatoes, bell peppers, and onion slices in a serving bowl or on a serving platter and toss together to mix. Scatter the sun-dried tomatoes over the top.

3 Place the yogurt, mayonnaise, mustard, parsley, and seasoning in a small bowl and mix thoroughly.

4 Sprinkle the dressing over the tomato-and-pepper salad and toss lightly to mix. Garnish with fresh parsley sprigs and serve with broiled lean meat or fish kabobs and warm pita bread.

VARIATION
● Use standard red tomatoes if yellow tomatoes are not available.

NUTRITIONAL ANALYSIS

(figures are per serving)

Calories = 107
Fat = 3.9g
of which saturates = 0.6g
    monounsaturates = 0.9g
    polyunsaturates = 2.2g
Protein = 3.5g
Carbohydrate = 15.1g
Dietary fiber = 3.0g
Sodium = 0.2g

Percentage of total calories from fat = 33%
of which saturates = 2%
Good source of vitamins A, C, & E

CURRIED CHICK-PEA & BROWN RICE SALAD

A blend of aromatic spices brings exotic flavor to this rice salad. Serve with fresh multi-grain bread rolls and mixed salad leaves.

Preparation time: 15 minutes
Cooking time: 20 minutes

Serves 6

1 cup mixed brown and wild rice
1 tsp olive oil
1 clove garlic, crushed
1 tsp ground coriander (cilantro)
1 tsp ground cumin
1 tsp turmeric
$^1/_2$ tsp hot chili powder
$^2/_3$ cup fresh tomato juice
2 tbsp red wine vinegar
1 tbsp tomato ketchup
salt and freshly ground black pepper
1 cup broccoli flowerets
3 tbsp minced parsley
1 tbsp chopped fresh thyme
2 bunches green onions (scallions), chopped
2 x 14-ounce cans chick-peas (garbanzo beans), rinsed and drained
$^3/_4$ cup yellow raisins

1 Cook the rice in a large saucepan of lightly salted, boiling water for about 20 minutes, or according to the package instructions, until the rice is cooked and just tender. Drain thoroughly and keep hot.

2 Meanwhile, make the dressing. Heat the oil in a saucepan, add the garlic and spices, and cook gently for 2 minutes, stirring.

3 Add the passata, vinegar, tomato ketchup, and seasoning and mix well. Heat gently, stirring occasionally, until the mixture comes to the boil. Keep the dressing warm.

4 Cook the broccoli in a saucepan of lightly salted, boiling water for about 5 minutes, until just tender. Drain thoroughly.

5 Place the cooked rice in a bowl, add the spicy tomato dressing, and stir to mix. Add the cooked broccoli and the remaining ingredients and toss together to mix.

6 Serve the rice salad warm or cold.

VARIATIONS

● Use brown or white rice in place of the brown and wild rice mix.
● Use other canned beans such as kidney beans or pinto beans in place of the chick-peas (garbanzo beans).
● Use chopped ready-to-eat dried apricots, peaches, or pears in place of the yellow raisins.

NUTRITIONAL ANALYSIS

(figures are per serving)

Calories = 372
Fat = 5.2g
of which saturates = 0.8g
    monounsaturates = 1.5g
    polyunsaturates = 2g
Protein = 12.9g
Carbohydrate = 73g
Dietary fiber = 6.9g
Sodium = 0.3g

Percentage of total calories from fat = 13%
of which saturates = 2%

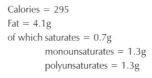

WARM
PASTA SALAD

This warm whole-wheat pasta salad, with zucchini and mushrooms tossed in a lightly spiced tomato dressing, makes an ideal dish for lunch or dinner.

Preparation time: 10 minutes

Cooking time: 10-12 minutes

Serves 4

12 ounces whole-wheat pasta shapes
2 tsp olive oil
1 clove garlic, crushed
1 bunch green onions (scallions), chopped
3 green zucchini, thinly sliced
3 yellow zucchini or summer squash, thinly sliced
2 cups sliced mushrooms
1¼ cups tomato juice or crushed tomatoes
1 tsp chili powder
salt and freshly ground black pepper
2 tbsp chopped fresh mixed herbs

1 Cook the pasta in a large saucepan of lightly salted, boiling water for 10-12 minutes, until just cooked or *al dente*.

2 Meanwhile, heat the oil in a large nonstick skillet or wok. Add the garlic and stir-fry over a medium heat for 30 seconds.

3 Add the green onions (scallions), zucchini, and mushrooms and stir-fry for about 5 minutes, until just cooked.

4 Add the tomato juice or crushed tomatoes, chili powder, and seasoning, and stir-fry until the tomato juice is hot and bubbling.

5 Drain the pasta thoroughly. Toss the pasta and zucchini mixture together until well mixed and sprinkle with the fresh herbs.

6 Serve immediately with slices of fresh, crusty bread.

NUTRITIONAL ANALYSIS

(figures are per serving)

Calories = 295	Protein = 12.3g
Fat = 4.1g	Carbohydrate = 55.6g
of which saturates = 0.7g	Dietary fiber = 5.1g
monounsaturates = 1.3g	Sodium = 0.01g
polyunsaturates = 1.3g	

Percentage of total calories from fat = 12%
of which saturates = 2%

VARIATIONS

● Use other mixtures of vegetables such as carrots and bell peppers in place of the zucchini and mushrooms.

● Use white or flavored pasta in place of the whole-wheat pasta.

● Use ground cumin or curry powder in place of the chili powder.

MULTI-COLORED
MIXED-BEAN SALAD

A colorful salad that is equally appetizing served warm or cold.

Preparation time: 10 minutes

Cooking time: 10 minutes

Serves 4

1 cup green beans, trimmed and halved
14-ounce can black-eyed peas, rinsed and drained
14-ounce can red kidney beans, rinsed and drained
14-ounce can chick-peas (garbanzo beans), rinsed and drained
1 sweet onion, chopped
1 yellow bell pepper, seeded and diced
2 tsp olive oil
2 cloves garlic, crushed
1 small red chili, seeded and finely chopped
²/₃ cup tomato juice
2 tbsp tomato ketchup
2 tbsp wine vinegar
2 tsp American mustard
few drops of Tabasco sauce
salt and freshly ground black pepper

1 Cook the green beans in a saucepan of lightly salted, boiling water for about 5 minutes, until just tender. Drain and cool.

2 Place the cooked green beans, black-eyed peas, red kidney beans, and chick-peas (garbanzo beans) in a bowl and stir together to mix. Add the onion and bell pepper and mix well.

3 Heat the oil in a saucepan, add the garlic and chili, and cook for 1 minute, stirring. Add all the remaining ingredients, mix well, and heat gently until boiling, stirring occasionally.

4 Pour the hot dressing over the beans and toss the ingredients together to mix.

5 Serve warm or cold with warmed pita bread or fresh crusty bread.

The dressing is suitable for cooking in a microwave oven.

VARIATIONS
● Use a different combination of beans such as pinto beans and lima beans.
● Use cider or tarragon vinegar in place of the wine vinegar.
● Use 1 red or orange bell pepper in place of the yellow bell pepper.
● Use 1 tsp chili powder in place of the fresh chili.
● Use whole-grain mustard in place of the American mustard.

NUTRITIONAL ANALYSIS
(figures are per serving)

Calories = 276

Fat = 5g

of which saturates = 0.6g

monounsaturates = 1.9g

polyunsaturates = 1.7g

Protein = 16.3g

Carbohydrate = 43.9g

Dietary fiber = 13.1g

Sodium = 1g

Percentage of total calories from fat = 16%, of which saturates = 2%

Good source of fiber & vitamin C

HERBS

Herbs, the aromatic and fragrant plants that many of us use to add flavor and color to our dishes, have been cultivated all over the world for centuries.

In cooking, herbs are chosen mainly for their flavoring and seasoning properties, and by combining and contrasting the different flavors of herbs, you will be able to enliven and enhance even the plainest dishes and make them into something special.

The flavor of an herb comes from the essential oils stored in the leaves, stems, flowers, seeds, or roots of the plant, which are released through heat or when the herb is cut or crushed.

As well as enhancing foods, some herbs provide valuable nutrients. For example, parsley provides a rich balance of vitamins and minerals. Herbs are also very low in fat and calories, so by using them you are able to add plenty of flavor and color to food without adding many calories or fats.

Use fresh herbs in generous amounts, either chopped and incorporated into a recipe or as an attractive garnish to a dish.

Dried herbs have a more concentrated flavor and are not as bright in color as fresh herbs. In recipes, 1 tbsp fresh herbs is roughly equal to 1 tsp dried herbs. Strongly flavored herbs, both fresh and dried, should be used sparingly.

Some herbs are added at the beginning of the cooking time, whereas others are added at the end, so that they don't lose their flavor or color. For example, rosemary sprigs and bay leaves are often added at the start of cooking to slowly release their wonderful flavors and aromas into the food. Other herbs, such as parsley and dill, are usually added just before food is served to give maximum flavor and color to the dish.

Remember, sprigs or leaves of fresh herbs make a lovely garnish and add the perfect finishing touch to any dish — both sweet and savory.

Try experimenting with the numerous herbs available, to create a whole variety of delightful flavors.

CARROT & RAISIN COLESLAW

Preparation time: 15 minutes
Serves 6

2 cups finely shredded white cabbage
³/₄ cup finely shredded red cabbage
1¹/₄ cups coarsely grated carrots
³/₄ cup raisins
¹/₂ cup low-fat plain yogurt
6 tbsp reduced-calorie mayonnaise
1-2 tbsp whole-grain mustard
2-3 tbsp chopped fresh parsley
salt and freshly ground black pepper

1 Place the white cabbage, red cabbage, carrots, and raisins in a bowl and mix well.

2 Place the yogurt, mayonnaise, mustard, parsley, and seasoning in a small bowl and mix thoroughly.

3 Spoon the mayonnaise mixture over the cabbage and toss the ingredients together to mix.

4 Serve immediately, or cover and chill in the refrigerator until ready to serve.

5 Serve with cooked, lean sliced meat.

NUTRITIONAL ANALYSIS

(figures are per serving)

Calories = 175
Fat = 5.3g
of which saturates = 0.7g
   monounsaturates = 1.3g
   polyunsaturates = 2.9g
Protein = 3.6g
Carbohydrate = 30g
Dietary fiber = 3.5g
Sodium = 0.3g

Percentage of total calories from fat = 27%
of which saturates = 4%
Good source of vitamins A & C

ROASTED
VEGETABLES

The flavors and colors of crisp Mediterranean-style vegetables are combined in this delicious and nutritious recipe, ideal for serving with broiled lean meat or fish and baked potatoes or pasta.

Preparation time: 10 minutes

Cooking time: 20-30 minutes

Serves 4

1 red onion, sliced
1 white or yellow onion, sliced
4 zucchini, thickly sliced
8 ounces baby corn
1 eggplant, cut into chunks
1 red bell pepper, seeded and cut into large dice
1 yellow bell pepper, seeded and cut into large dice
2 cloves garlic, thinly sliced
4 tsp olive oil
salt and freshly ground black pepper
2-3 tbsp chopped fresh mixed herbs

1 Place all the vegetables and garlic in a nonstick roasting pan and mix together.

2 Add the oil and seasoning and toss until the vegetables are lightly coated with oil.

3 Bake in a preheated oven at 425° for 20-30 minutes, until just tender and tinged brown at the edges, stirring once or twice.

4 Sprinkle with the herbs and toss to mix. Serve hot or cold with broiled lean meat or fish and baked potatoes.

VARIATIONS
● Use flavored olive oil such as chili oil or herb oil.
● Use other chopped fresh herbs such as parsley, chives, or rosemary in place of the mixed herbs.
● Sprinkle the vegetables with red wine vinegar or herb vinegar just before serving.

NUTRITIONAL ANALYSIS
(figures are per serving)

Calories = 116

Fat = 4.2g

of which saturates = 0.6g

monounsaturates = 2.2g

polyunsaturates = 0.7g

Protein = 5.6g

Carbohydrate = 14.6g

Dietary fiber = 5.3g

Sodium = 0.6g

Percentage of total calories from fat = 33%

of which saturates = 5%

Good source of vitamins A & C

SAUTÉED ROOT VEGETABLES

Root vegetables are full of their own natural flavors and combine well with fresh rosemary and seasoning.

Preparation time: 20 minutes

Cooking time: 20 minutes

Serves 4

12 ounces potatoes
1 medium sweet potato
1 small jicama
1 small rutabaga
3 carrots
1 celery root
1 tbsp olive oil
1 onion, chopped
2 cloves garlic, crushed
1-2 tbsp finely chopped fresh rosemary
salt and freshly ground black pepper
fresh rosemary sprigs, to garnish

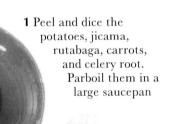

1 Peel and dice the potatoes, jicama, rutabaga, carrots, and celery root. Parboil them in a large saucepan of lightly salted, boiling water for 5 minutes. Drain thoroughly.

2 Heat the oil in a large nonstick skillet, add the onion and garlic, and cook for 1 minute, stirring.

3 Add the diced vegetables, chopped rosemary, and seasoning, and mix well. Cook over a medium heat, turning over frequently, until the vegetables are cooked, lightly browned, and crispy.

4 Garnish with fresh rosemary sprigs and serve hot with broiled fish such as salmon or rainbow trout and fresh seasonal vegetables such as broccoli flowerets and baby carrots.

VARIATION
● Use 1 red onion or 6 shallots in place of the onion, for a change.

NUTRITIONAL ANALYSIS

(figures are per serving)

Calories = 205
Fat = 4.1g
of which saturates = 0.6g
      monounsaturates = 2.2g
      polyunsaturates = 0.7g
Protein = 4.7g
Carbohydrate = 39.6g
Dietary fiber = 8.2g
Sodium = 0.09g

Percentage of total calories from fat = 18%
of which saturates = 3%
Good source of vitamin A

STIR-FRIED JULIENNE OF VEGETABLES

Preparation time: 10 minutes

Cooking time: 5 minutes

Serves 4

2 tsp olive oil
3 zucchini, cut into matchstick (julienne) strips
4 carrots, cut into matchstick strips
1 red bell pepper, seeded and sliced into strips
1 yellow bell pepper, seeded and sliced into strips
juice of 1 lemon
salt and freshly ground black pepper
2 tbsp chopped fresh mixed herbs

1 Heat the oil in a large nonstick skillet or wok. Add the zucchini, carrots, and bell peppers and stir-fry over a high heat for 4-5 minutes, until just tender.

2 Add the lemon juice and seasoning and stir-fry for 30-60 seconds.

3 Add the herbs, toss together to mix, and serve immediately.

VARIATION
● Use the juice of 1 lime or 1 orange in place of the lemon juice.

NUTRITIONAL ANALYSIS

(figures are per serving)

Calories = 84
Fat = 2.4g
of which saturates = 0.4g
      monounsaturates = 1.1g
      polyunsaturates = 0.6g
Protein = 3g
Carbohydrate = 13.3g
Dietary fiber = 4.3g
Sodium = 0.03g

Percentage of total calories from fat = 25%
of which saturates = 5%
Good source of vitamins A & C

DESSERTS

*D*esserts are often the part of a meal that people most look forward to. Even if you are watching your intake of calories and fat, there is no need to miss out. You can still indulge and enjoy something sweet without having to feel guilty about eating a calorie- and fat-laden dessert. Here is a tempting selection of mouthwatering desserts that exploit the full flavor potential of ripe, fresh fruits, as well as versatile dried fruits and convenient canned fruits. Enjoy these light desserts whenever you like as part of a healthy diet.

RED SUMMER FRUIT
ROULADE

In this sumptuous dessert, an airy sponge is filled with a creamy yogurt mixture and luscious fresh berries.

Preparation time: 25 minutes, plus cooling time

Cooking time: 10-12 minutes

Serves 8

3 eggs
²/₃ cup sugar
finely grated rind of 1 lemon
1 cup all-purpose flour
²/₃ cup reduced-fat sour cream
²/₃ cup low-fat plain yogurt
³/₄ cup sliced strawberries
³/₄ cup red or black raspberries

1 Lightly grease a 13 x 9-inch jellyroll pan and line it with nonstick baking paper.

2 Place the eggs and ¹/₂ cup of the sugar in a large bowl and stand the bowl over a saucepan of hot water.

3 Using an electric whisk, whisk the mixture until pale and creamy, and thick enough to leave a trail on the surface of the mixture when the whisk is lifted out.

4 Remove the bowl from the saucepan and whisk until cool. Add the lemon rind, sift the flour over the mixture, and gently fold them in using a metal spoon. Gently fold in 1 tbsp hot water.

5 Pour the mixture into the pan and tilt to spread the mixture evenly.

6 Bake in a preheated oven at 40° for 10-12 minutes, until well-risen, golden brown, and firm to the touch.

7 Meanwhile, sprinkle a sheet of nonstick baking paper or parchment paper with the remaining sugar. Quickly turn the cake out onto the paper, trim off the crusty edges, and roll the cake up loosely with the paper inside. Place, seam downward, on a wire rack to cool.

8 Fold together the yogurt and sour cream. When the cake is cool, unroll it and spread the yogurt mixture over the cake, not quite to the edges. Scatter the strawberries and raspberries over the top.

9 Roll up the roulade, place it on a serving plate, seam downward, slice, and serve immediately.

The baked jellyroll without the filling is suitable for freezing.

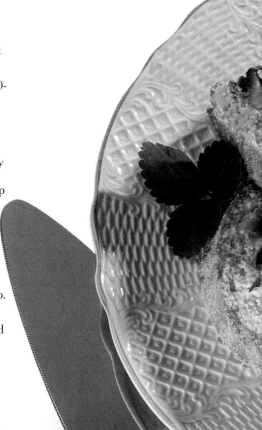

QUICK CHERRY
BRULÉE

*A quick and light dessert that is sure to satisfy those
sweet-loving tastebuds every time.*

Preparation time: 10 minutes, plus chilling time

Serves 4

NUTRITIONAL ANALYSIS

(figures are per serving)

Calories = 196
Fat = 5.4g
of which saturates = 2.3g
     monounsaturates = 1.9g
     polyunsaturates = 0.5g
Protein = 6.9g
Carbohydrate = 32.1g
Dietary fiber = 0.9g
Sodium = 0.05g

Percentage of total calories from fat = 25%
of which saturates = 10%

1¹/₄ cups low-fat plain yogurt
²/₃ cup reduced-fat sour cream
14-ounce can cherries in syrup, drained
2 tbsp light soft brown sugar
fresh mint sprigs, to decorate
1 pound fresh cherries

1 Combine the yogurt and sour cream.
Place half the canned cherries in a
serving bowl.

2 Spread half the yogurt mixture over the
cherries and sprinkle with half the sugar.

3 Repeat the layers with the remaining
cherries, yogurt mixture, and sugar,
ending with a layer of sugar.

4 Cover and chill for several hours
before serving. Decorate with fresh mint
sprigs and serve with fresh cherries.

VARIATIONS

● This dessert may be made and served
in individual sundae glasses.
● Use other canned fruit in fruit juice
such as peaches, apricots, or raspberries
in place of the cherries.
● Use dark brown sugar in place of the
light soft brown sugar.

NUTRITIONAL ANALYSIS

(figures are per serving)

Calories = 271
Fat = 6.7g
of which saturates = 3.8g
     monounsaturates = 1.9g
     polyunsaturates = 0.4g
Protein = 7.9g
Carbohydrate = 48.2g
Dietary fiber = 1.6g
Sodium = 0.04g

Percentage of total calories from fat = 23%
of which saturates = 10%

DRIED FRUIT PURÉES

An excellent way to reduce your fat intake yet still enjoy delicious, home-baked cakes is to use an easy-to-make natural sugar substitute in the form of a dried fruit purée. Dried fruit purées such as apricot or prune purée may even be used to replace the fat in some cake recipes. They are most suited to cakes which require a moist texture and a fruity flavor. Dried fruit purées are not suitable for replacing the fat in recipes such as sponge cakes, yellow cakes, or pastry.

By substituting dried fruit purée for butter, margarine, or oil, you are able to cut down the fat content of some cake recipes quite dramatically, as well as reducing the calories. Dried fruit purées also contribute additional nutrients to your diet, including dietary fiber, iron, and vitamin A.

Dried fruit purées are very simple to make and are easy to use. To make a fruit purée, roughly chop about ³/₄ cup ready-to-eat dried apricots. Place them in a liquidizer or food processor with 5 tbsp water and blend until fairly smooth — the consistency of cooked oatmeal.

To use the dried fruit purée in place of fat, simply substitute fruit purée for the same amount of butter, margarine, or oil in the original recipe. For example, if a recipe calls for ³/₄ cup butter or margarine, use ³/₄ cup ready-to-eat dried apricots or prunes, puréed with 5 tbsp water (as above), in place of the fat.

As an alternative, you may wish to use a combination of half dried fruit purée and half fat in place of the normal weight of fat in some recipes — this would still make a considerable reduction in the fat content.

Experiment with your own recipes at home and try using other dried fruit purées in place of the apricot and prune purées — you'll be pleasantly surprised at the results!

APRICOT & CINNAMON
RAISIN SQUARES

Apricot purée replaces the fat in this recipe but you won't miss out on anything! Enjoy these moist cakes on their own as a snack with a piece of fresh fruit, or with low-fat topping or ice cream for a delicious dessert.

Preparation time: 15 minutes

Cooking time: 30-35 minutes

Makes 16 squares

³/₄ cup ready-to-eat dried apricots
1 cup self-rising flour, sifted
¹/₄ tsp baking powder
2 tsp ground cinnamon
³/₄ cup light soft brown sugar
2 eggs, beaten
¹/₂ cup yellow raisins
3 tbsp freshly squeezed orange juice
2 tbsp granulated sugar

1 Chop the apricots coarsely and place them in a liquidizer or food processor with 5 tbsp water. Blend until they are the consistency of cooked oatmeal.

2 Place the apricot purée, flour, baking powder, cinnamon, soft brown sugar, and eggs in a bowl and beat together until thoroughly mixed. Stir in the yellow raisins and mix well.

3 Turn the mixture into a lightly greased 7-inch square cake pan and level the surface.

4 Bake in a preheated oven at 350° for 30-35 minutes, until risen, golden brown, and firm to the touch.

5 Mix the orange juice and granulated sugar together and pour the mixture evenly over the hot cake.

6 Using a sharp knife, mark the cake into squares while it is still hot and allow to cool in the pan for 10 minutes. Cut the cake into squares and transfer to a wire rack to cool completely.

7 Once cool, store these cakes in an airtight container at room temperature.

VARIATIONS
● Add the finely grated rind of 1 small orange to the cake mixture before baking.
● Use other ground spices such as ginger or mixed spice in place of the cinnamon.
● Use lemon juice for the cake topping.
● If self-rising flour is not available, use all-purpose flour with double the quantity of double-acting baking powder and 1 tsp baking soda.

CHOCOLATE RAISIN SQUARES
Follow the recipe above but omit the cinnamon, use ³/₄ cup raisins in place of the yellow raisins, and add 2 ounces (2 squares) melted baking chocolate to the cake mixture in Step 2 before stirring in the raisins.

NUTRITIONAL ANALYSIS

(figures are per square)

Calories = 102
Fat = 0.9g
of which saturates = 0.2g
monounsaturates = 0.3g
polyunsaturates = 0.1g
Protein = 2g
Carbohydrate = 23.2g
Dietary fiber = 0.8g
Sodium = 0.04g

Percentage of total calories from fat = 8%
of which saturates = 2%

PINEAPPLE UPSIDE-DOWN
CAKE

*A reduced-fat version of an old favorite, this upside-down cake comprises a
light sponge topped with a layer of juicy fruit.*

Preparation time: 20 minutes

Cooking time: 45 minutes

Serves 6

6 tbsp dark corn syrup
8-ounce can pineapple rings in fruit juice, drained
9 ready-to-eat dried apricots
1/2 cup low-fat spread
1/2 cup sugar
2 eggs
1 1/2 cups self-rising flour
1 tsp baking powder
1 tsp ground cinnamon
3 tbsp unsweetened pineapple juice

● Use other dried fruits such as prunes
or candied cherries in place of the
apricots, for added variety.
● Omit the cinnamon, if preferred.

1 Lightly grease the base of a 7-inch
round cake pan and line it with nonstick
baking paper. Heat the syrup in a
saucepan and boil it until it is slightly
reduced. Pour it into the prepared pan to
cover the bottom.

2 Arrange the pineapple rings and
apricots in the syrup.

3 Place the low-fat spread, sugar, and
eggs in a bowl. Sift the flour, baking
powder, and cinnamon into the bowl and
then add the pineapple juice.

4 Beat the mixture thoroughly, using an
electric mixer or wooden spoon, until
smooth and creamy.

5 Spread the cake mixture evenly over
the fruit. Bake in a preheated oven at
350° for about 45 minutes until well-risen,
golden brown, and firm to the touch.

6 Unmold onto a warmed serving platter
and serve in slices with low-fat yogurt or
reduced-fat cream.

VARIATIONS
● Replace 2 tbsp of the flour with sifted
cocoa powder.
● Use other canned fruits such as pears
or apricots in place of the pineapple.

APPLE
PUDDING

This chunky apple pudding, subtly flavored with cinnamon and served with low-fat topping, is sure to become a family favorite.

Preparation time: 15 minutes

Cooking time: 1-1¼ hours

Serves 6

½ cup low-fat spread
½ cup light soft brown sugar
2 eggs
1½ cups self-rising flour, sifted
1 tsp baking powder, sifted
1 tsp ground cinnamon
3 tbsp skim milk
3 tart dessert apples
2 tbsp yellow raisins
2 tbsp dark raisins

1 Place the low-fat spread, sugar, eggs, flour, baking powder, cinnamon, and milk in a bowl. Beat the mixture thoroughly, using an electric mixer or wooden spoon, until smooth.

2 Peel, core, and dice the apples, add to the cake mixture with the yellow and dark raisins, and mix well.

3 Transfer the mixture to a lightly greased ovenproof dish and bake in a preheated oven at 350° for 1-1¼ hours, until risen, golden brown, and firm to the touch.

4 Serve hot with low-fat topping or ice cream.

VARIATIONS
● Use peaches in place of the apples.
● Use white granulated sugar in place of the brown sugar.
● If self-rising flour is not available, use all-purpose flour, or half all-purpose and half whole-wheat flour, with double the quantity of double-acting baking powder and 1 tsp baking soda

NUTRITIONAL ANALYSIS

(figures are per serving)

Calories = 336
Fat = 10.3g
of which saturates = 2.8g
    monounsaturates = 4.3g
    polyunsaturates = 2.3g

Protein = 6.9g
Carbohydrate = 58.4g
Dietary fiber = 1.9g
Sodium = 0.3g

Percentage of total calories from fat = 28%
of which saturates = 7%

HONEY-BAKED
FRUIT

Preparation time: 15 minutes

Cooking time: 30 minutes

Serves 4

8-ounce can pineapple chunks
in fruit juice
4 tbsp clear honey
½ tsp ground mixed spice
2 dessert apples, peeled, cored, and sliced
2 pears, peeled, cored, and sliced
2 peaches, peeled, pitted, and sliced
2 bananas, peeled and cut into chunks

1 Drain the pineapple, reserving the juice and fruit separately. Place the pineapple juice in a bowl with the honey and spice and mix well.

2 Place the prepared fresh fruits in an ovenproof dish and stir to mix.

3 Pour the honey mixture over the fruits and stir to mix. Cover and bake in a preheated oven at 350° for about 30 minutes, until the fruit is just beginning to soften.

4 Serve hot with low-fat ice cream or reduced-fat cream.

NUTRITIONAL ANALYSIS

(figures are per serving)

Calories = 211
Fat = 0.3g
of which saturates = 0g
    monounsaturates = 0g
    polyunsaturates = 0.1g
Protein = 1.8g
Carbohydrate = 53.4g
Dietary fiber = 3.9g
Sodium = 0g

Percentage of total calories from fat = 1%
of which saturates = 0%
Good source of vitamin C

NECTARINE
CHOUX RING

*This light and crispy choux pastry ring, filled with
a creamy combination of low-fat yogurt and topping and topped with fresh
fruit, is sure to impress your family or guests.*

Preparation time: 25 minutes, plus cooling time

Cooking time: 40 minutes

Serves 6

NUTRITIONAL ANALYSIS

(figures are per serving)

Calories = 200
Fat = 7.9g
of which saturates = 2.7g
      monounsaturates = 2.9g
      polyunsaturates = 1.3g
Protein = 8.1g
Carbohydrate = 25.5g
Dietary fiber = 2.4g
Sodium = 0.1g

Percentage of total calories from fat = 35%
of which saturates = 10%
Good source of vitamin C

4 tbsp low-fat spread
5 tbsp all-purpose flour
2 eggs, beaten
²/₃ cup low-fat yogurt
*²/₃ cup low-fat ready-made vanilla-flavored dessert
topping*
4 nectarines or peaches, peeled, pitted, and sliced
1 cup raspberries
1 tbsp powdered (confectioner's) sugar, to decorate
fresh mint sprigs, to decorate

1 Line a cookie sheet with nonstick
baking paper.

2 Place the low-fat spread in a saucepan
with ²/₃ cup water. Heat gently until
the spread has melted, then bring to
the boil.

3 Remove the pan from the heat, quickly
add the flour, and beat well until the
mixture is smooth and leaves the sides
of the pan. Allow the mixture to
cool slightly.

4 Gradually beat in the eggs, using a
wooden spoon, until the mixture is
smooth and shiny.

5 Drop spoonfuls of the dough onto the
paper on the cookie sheet to form a ring,
making sure they are just touching.

6 Bake in a preheated oven at 400° for
about 40 minutes, until risen, golden
brown, and crisp.

7 Immediately slice the ring horizontally
in half to release the steam inside, and
return to the oven for about 5 minutes to
dry out. Carefully transfer to a wire rack
to cool.

8 Place the bottom half of the choux ring
on a serving platter. Combine the yogurt
and dessert topping and spoon the
mixture into the ring.

9 Top with the prepared fruits, then
place the top of the choux ring over
the fruit.

10 Sift the powdered (confectioner's)
sugar over the choux ring, decorate
with mint sprigs, and fill the centre
of the ring with extra raspberries,
if you like. Serve immediately
in slices.

VARIATION
● Use other
prepared fresh or
canned fruits
such as apricots
and strawberries
in place of the
nectarines and
raspberries.

PROFITEROLES

A light version of this popular dessert, delicious served with fresh fruit such as strawberries, makes a perfect finale for a family feast or special-occasion meal.

Preparation time: 30 minutes, plus cooling time
Cooking time: 15-20 minutes
Serves 6

4 tbsp low-fat spread
5 tbsp all-purpose flour, sifted
2 eggs, beaten

FOR THE CHOCOLATE SAUCE
2¹/₂ ounces (2¹/₂ squares) baking chocolate, broken into pieces
6 tbsp dark corn syrup

1 cup low-fat vanilla ice cream or frozen dessert
1 pound strawberries
strawberry or mint leaves, to decorate

1 Line two cookie sheets with nonstick baking paper.

2 Place the low-fat spread in a saucepan with ²/₃ cup water. Heat gently until the spread has melted, then bring to the boil.

3 Remove the pan from the heat, quickly add the flour, and beat well until the mixture is smooth and leaves the sides of the pan. Allow the mixture to cool slightly.

4 Gradually beat in the eggs, using a wooden spoon, until the mixture is smooth and shiny. Spoon the mixture into a piping bag fitted with a medium-sized plain nozzle. Pipe walnut-sized balls of the mixture onto the prepared cookie sheets.

5 Bake in a preheated oven at 400° for 15-20 minutes, until crisp and golden.

6 With a sharp, pointed knife, carefully slice the top off each profiterole to allow steam to escape. Transfer to a wire rack to cool completely.

7 Meanwhile, make the chocolate sauce. Place the chocolate and syrup in a bowl over a pan of simmering water and stir until melted and well blended.

8 Spoon some ice cream into each profiterole and cover with the tops.

9 To serve, pile the profiteroles into small pyramids on individual serving plates. Arrange some strawberries on each plate. Pour some of the sauce over the profiteroles and strawberries, and serve with the remaining sauce handed separately. Decorate with strawberry or mint leaves.

VARIATIONS
● Use milk, white, orange, or mint-flavored chocolate in place of the baking chocolate, for variety.
● Use other flavored low-fat ice cream or frozen deserts such as strawberry or chocolate in place of the vanilla ice cream.
● A melon-baller is an ideal tool for scooping small portions of ice cream to fill the profiteroles.

NUTRITIONAL ANALYSIS

(figures are per serving)

Calories = 286
Fat = 9.4g
of which saturates = 3.6g
     monounsaturates = 3.6g
     polyunsaturates = 1.3g
Protein = 6g
Carbohydrate = 47.1g
Dietary fiber = 1.5g
Sodium = 0.2g

Percentage of total calories from fat = 30%
of which saturates = 10%
Good source of vitamin C

RASPBERRY MERINGUE NESTS

This is a simple but highly attractive dessert. Crispy meringue nests contrast with a creamy yogurt filling topped with fresh raspberries.

Preparation time: 25 minutes, plus cooling time
Cooking time: 2½-3 hours
Serves 6

3 egg whites
³/₄ cup sugar
³/₄ cup low-fat yogurt
1 cup black or red raspberries
fresh mint sprigs, to decorate

1 Line two cookie sheets with nonstick baking paper. Draw six 4-inch circles on the paper and turn over.

2 Place the egg whites in a bowl and whisk until stiff. Gradually whisk in half the sugar, whisking well after each addition.

3 Gradually whisk in the remaining sugar until well incorporated.

4 Spoon the meringue into a piping bag fitted with a large star nozzle. Pipe a continuous coil of meringue on each circle on the paper to make the bases, then pipe an extra ring of meringue on top of each circle around the edge to make a nest or basket shape.

5 Bake in a preheated oven at 225° for 2½-3 hours, until crisp and dry.

6 Leave to cool on a wire rack, then peel off the base paper. Place the meringue nests on serving plates.

7 Spoon some yogurt into each nest and top with some raspberries. Serve immediately, decorated with mint sprigs.

VARIATION
● Use different prepared fresh fruit.

NUTRITIONAL ANALYSIS

(figures are per serving)

Calories = 164
Fat = 2.8g
of which saturates = 1.6g
     monounsaturates = 0.8g
     polyunsaturates = 0.2g
Protein = 3.8g
Carbohydrate = 32.9g
Dietary fiber = 0.9g
Sodium = 0.05g

Percentage of total calories from fat = 15%
of which saturates = 8%

SPICED APPLE STRUDEL

*A popular choice for a dessert, this elegant strudel is perfect
for entertaining or for a special-occasion family meal.*

Preparation time: 25 minutes

Cooking time: 40 minutes

Serves 8

*1³/₄ pounds tart apples, such as Baldwin,
Cortland, or Newtown
finely grated rind and juice of 1 lemon
2 tbsp yellow raisins
2 tbsp dark raisins
2 tbsp ready-to-eat dried apricots, chopped
2 tbsp light soft brown sugar
2 tsp ground mixed spice
4 sheets phyllo dough (each about 18 x 10 inches)
2 tbsp sunflower oil
4 tbsp fresh white bread crumbs
1 tbsp powdered (confectioner's) sugar*

1 Peel, core, and slice the apples.
Place them in a bowl with the lemon
rind and juice, raisins, apricots, sugar,
and spice and mix well.

2 Place 1 sheet of phyllo dough on a
sheet of nonstick baking paper and
brush the dough lightly with oil.

3 Place another sheet on top, brush
lightly with oil, and layer the
remaining 2 sheets of dough on top,
brushing each one lightly with oil.

4 Sprinkle the bread crumbs over the
dough, leaving a 1-inch border all
around the edge.

5 Spread the apple mixture evenly
over the bread crumbs, then fold the
border edges over the fruit mixture.

6 With one long side toward you,
using the nonstick baking paper,
carefully roll up the strudel.

7 Place the strudel seam-side down on
a cookie sheet lined with parchment
paper. If the oven or cookie sheet is too
small to take the strudel in a long roll,
curve it into a horseshoe shape. Brush
the strudel all over lightly with oil.

8 Bake in a preheated oven at
375° for about 40 minutes, until crisp
and golden.

9 Dust with sifted powdered
(confectioner's) sugar just before
serving and serve hot or cold cut into
slices with low-fat ice cream or
reduced-fat cream.

NUTRITIONAL ANALYSIS

(figures are per serving)

Calories = 198
Fat = 3.7g
of which saturates = 0.4g
     monounsaturates = 0.6g
     polyunsaturates = 1.9g
Protein = 3.5g
Carbohydrate = 40g
Dietary fiber = 2.3g
Sodium = 0.2g

Percentage of total calories from fat = 17%
of which saturates = 2%

STRAWBERRY YOGURT ICE

A refreshing iced dessert, easy to make and delicious served as a light dessert on its own or with fresh fruit or vanilla wafers.

Preparation time: 10 minutes, plus freezing time
Serves 6

1 pound strawberries
¹/₂ cup sugar
1¹/₄ cups low-fat strawberry yogurt
1¹/₄ reduced-fat sour cream
strawberry leaves and strawberries, or other berries, to decorate

1 Place the strawberries in a liquidizer or food processor and blend until smooth.

2 Add the sugar, yogurts and sour cream and blend until well mixed.

3 Pour the mixture into a shallow, plastic, freezer-proof container. Cover with plastic wrap and freeze for about 3 hours, or until the mixture is just frozen all over and is mushy in consistency.

4 Turn the mixture into a chilled bowl and mash with a fork to break down the ice crystals, beating until smooth.

5 Return to the container, cover, and freeze again for about 2 hours, or until mushy. Turn into a chilled bowl and mash again as before.

6 Return to the container, cover, and freeze until firm.

7 Place in the refrigerator for about 30 minutes before serving, to allow the yogurt ice to soften a little.

8 Serve in scoops, decorated with strawberry leaves and strawberries.

VARIATION

● Use other prepared fresh or canned fruit such as blueberries, loganberries, raspberries, peaches, or apricots in place of the strawberries.

NUTRITIONAL ANALYSIS

(figures are per serving)

Calories = 188	Protein = 6.1g
Fat = 3.2g	Carbohydrate = 35.9g
of which saturates = 1.8g	Dietary fiber = 0.8g
monounsaturates = 0.9g	Sodium = 0.04g
polyunsaturates = 0.2g	

Percentage of total calories from fat = 15%
of which saturates = 9%
Good source of vitamin C

OTHER YOGURT ICES

Yogurt ices are easy to make, and once you have mastered the basic strawberry yogurt ice recipe, you can easily adapt the recipe to make lots of other delicious flavors.

MANGO & LIME
Use peeled, chopped, ripe mango in place of the strawberries, and add the finely grated rind of 2 limes. Replace the strawberry-flavored yogurt with low-fat plain yogurt or 1¹/₄ cups low-fat soft cheese or small-curd cottage cheese.

MIXED BERRY
Use a mixture of fresh mixed berries such as strawberries, raspberries, and loganberries in place of the strawberries.

APRICOT OR TANGERINE
Use fresh or canned prepared apricots or tangerines in place of the strawberries and use low-fat apricot or tangerine yogurt in place of the strawberry yogurt.

CHERRY
Use fresh or canned prepared cherries in place of the strawberries and low-fat cherry yogurt or plain yogurt in place of the strawberry yogurt.